C000246982

TRIAL AN

Trial and Error

Mordechai Vanunu and Israel's Nuclear Bomb

Tom Gilling and John McKnight

HarperCollins*Publishers*

HarperCollins*Publishers*
77–85 Fulham Palace Road, London W6 8JB

First published in Great Britain in 1991 by Monarch Publications Ltd
Revised edition published in 1995 by HarperCollins*Publishers*

1   3   5   7   9   10   8   6   4   2

A catalogue record for this book is
available from the British Library

ISBN 0 00 627846-9

Printed and bound in Great Britain by
HarperCollinsManufacturing Glasgow

To know is to be responsible.

Mordechai Vanunu

CHAPTER ONE

SYDNEY WAS COOL AND CLOUDY on the night of Friday 23rd May, 1986. Mordechai Vanunu, wearing jeans and a checked shirt, was just one of many friendless people walking the streets of Darlinghurst. A hundred metres away, cars crawled slowly down William Street, their occupants eyeing the prostitutes who stood in fishnet stockings and leotards on every street corner. At the top of the hill a vast neon Coca-Cola advertisement flickered above the crowded main street of Kings Cross, with its fast-food restaurants and tacky souvenir shops and doorways scarcely wide enough for the bouncers who blocked them. Prostitutes lounged against shop windows or haggled in side streets. But on this side of the underpass the streets were dark, deserted except for the occasional figure carrying bags of washing to the launderette.

As Vanunu wandered past the large dilapidated rectory of St John's Anglican Church he noticed that the lights of the sandstone church were on. Outside were some tables and chairs for coffee, looked after by David Smith, the catechist, and Gillian Thornbury, a parishioner. The rector of St John's, John McKnight, was inside. The doors were open as part of Operation

7

Nicodemus, a scheme to open the church at night as a refuge for homeless teenagers and others who needed somewhere to escape from the streets. Vanunu walked down the short path to the door. What followed was to change the whole course of his life.

McKnight introduced himself and Vanunu started talking. He said he was Jewish. McKnight took him to the front of the church and pointed out the Star of David carved in the prayer desk and two others on the floor of the sanctuary area. Then, after chatting for about half an hour, he took Vanunu outside to join the others.

Vanunu seemed relaxed and curious, recalls David Smith, just like any other foreign tourist. Vanunu gave the impression that he had not been inside a church before, although he had actually visited several while travelling in Europe. As they talked outside over coffee, Vanunu expressed some of his deep disillusionment with Judaism, his scorn of Rabbis and their position in the state of Israel.

Vanunu, like David Smith, had studied philosophy at university. Despite his faltering grasp of English, he was very anxious to talk about his studies while in Israel. He especially wanted to talk about the ideas of the Danish philosopher Søren Kierkegaard, and told Smith that he had read *Fear and Trembling*, the only one of Kierkegaard's books to have been translated into Hebrew.

'We talked rather deeply in a funny way about various things on that first night,' recalls Smith. 'We talked of the Nietzschean idea of staring into the abyss and recognising despair as against Kierkegaard's idea of throwing yourself into the abyss and finding that the abyss is gone and God holds you up. We found a basic dichotomy between the Nietzschean idea of recognising the irrationality of life and seeing the pointlessness of it and simply embracing despair, and the Kierkegaardian idea of embracing God as the answer to life. Mordechai seemed trapped by a sense of despair.'

The seeds of Vanunu's disillusionment with Judaism were buried in the religious conservatism that Vanunu's father, like thousands of other poor Jewish immigrants, brought with him when he embarked on a new life in Israel. Mordechai Vanunu was nine when his family joined the hordes of migrants converging on the Jewish State from Morocco and other Arab countries. Moroccans formed the largest but also the poorest of the Jewish ethnic groups arriving to discover not the promised land they hoped for, but a series of raw and often squalid development towns in Israel's desolate empty spaces.

Moroccan Jews with money and education had settled in Canada and France, where they were able to find their way back into business and the professions. The poor, who migrated to Israel from the ghettos of Marrakesh and the Atlas Mountains, settled down with little complaint to the rough conditions afforded by the young country, grateful to have found a haven in the Jewish State, and to have escaped the uncertainty of life under Arab rule. Since the end of World War II, when the European powers began to disengage themselves from their North African and Middle Eastern colonies, the Jews had faced growing hostility from Arab nationalist governments. In the first five years of the State of Israel, successive waves of Jewish refugees had arrived from Iraq, Libya, Yemen, Morocco, Tunisia and Egypt. Ten years later, poor immigrants were still arriving in their thousands. The Vanunus were settled by the Government in Beersheba, where they took their place in one of the numerous cramped and anonymous apartments of what was officially named D neighbourhood.

Mordechai's father, Solomon Vanunu, was an Orthodox Jew, a devout man who earned his living selling religious artefacts in Beersheba market. Fellow worshippers at the synagogue he attended addressed

9

him as rabbi. He expected his children to grow up as Jews.

Mordechai was the second of eight children, a quiet, intelligent child whom his father described as 'a thinker—somebody people listened to'. When he was fourteen, Solomon enrolled him in the Wolfson Yeshiva religious school in Beersheba. Reports of his time at school suggest that he began well but slowly lost momentum.

A fellow student remembered him as becoming 'indifferent and withdrawn. It became necessary to make him do things, even to clean the yard when it was his turn on the roster.'

Describing this period of his childhood, Vanunu himself later wrote:

> I was born Jewish and grew up in a Jewish family, but when I was sixteen years old I was disappointed. I didn't like to keep the old laws without caring about human beings. At the same time, I started reading books and looking for my God, my Saviour. It was there in the New Testament, but I, like many other Jews, didn't have the chance to read, to know about the son of God, his life and his gospel.

This overwhelming sense of disappointment cut him off from his fellow students. He never attended high-school reunions or met with childhood friends. Descriptions of his solitary behaviour would later be seized upon by the Israeli press as evidence of a fundamentally unstable character. In fact, it reflected his growing dissatisfaction with the orthodox Jewish beliefs which had been instilled into him since a small boy. He began to despise the rabbinical system for what he saw as its hollow mouthing of old rhetoric and arcane laws that seemed out of touch with his view of the world. Later he was to describe rabbis as 'parasites on the state'. Vanunu had not discovered Christianity, but he was groping for something radically different from the religion of his father. He had already begun to cut his spiritual ties with Judaism.

Vanunu joined the Israeli army in 1972. Indifference bordering on alienation continued to mark him during his period of compulsory military service, yet he still reached the rank of first sergeant in a sapper unit on the Golan Heights. Fellow soldiers again described his behaviour as 'withdrawn', 'strange', even 'surly'. These reminiscences, gathered by the Israeli press in the full fury of the reaction against him, need to be treated with circumspection. If nothing else, they confirm that Vanunu had cut himself off from the mainstream of society.

After leaving the army, Vanunu entered Ramat Aviv University in Tel Aviv. He failed two exams after the first year of a physics course and returned home. Since he was to sail through later exams, and was considered to be bright enough to study for a master's degree in philosophy, this again suggests that the period was one of emotional and intellectual turmoil for him.

In the midsummer of 1976, Vanunu responded to an advertisement for a job as a trainee technician at what is officially known as Kirya-le-Mehekar Gariny, or KMG, a nuclear research centre run by the Israeli Atomic Energy Authority in the Negev Desert. He went on the payroll in November 1976. He was not taken to the reactor complex straightaway, but was sent back to school to do a crash course in physics, maths, chemistry and English. He passed the initial entrance exam with ease, and in February 1978 took his place on one of the blue-and-white Volvo buses bound for Dimona.

With the rest of his intake, Vanunu was taken to a school within the Dimona complex where he was required to sign the Israeli Official Secrets Act. He was handed a security pass, pronounced medically fit, and then put through a course on elementary nuclear physics and nuclear chemistry. Only then was he given the pass that would let him through the doors of Machon 2, the most secret part of the complex, where the bombs were manufactured. The new employees were given ten weeks to familiarise themselves with the labyrinth that extended deep underground beneath the windowless warehouse. They completed their initial training at the end of June. A sudden call-up for a month's army reserve duty with his engineer unit was cancelled as soon as the authorities discovered that Vanunu was on the staff at Dimona, and he was back inside Machon 2 within a week.

The final hurdle before Vanunu could begin work was an examination before a panel comprising one of the Dimona school lecturers, an independent engineer and a specialist in handling radio-active materials. Vanunu passed the test, and on 7th August 1977, he turned up for his first shift as a controller on the night shift in Machon 2, working from 11.30 pm until 8 am.

In 1978 Vanunu enrolled for a part-time degree course at Ben Gurion University, Beersheba, which he somehow managed to fit around his full-time job at Dimona. At this time he quickly earned a reputation for his extreme right-wing views, and was considered a 'Kahanist hawk', after Rabbi Meir Kahane, a right-wing, anti-Palestinian extremist. Vanunu studied geography and philosophy, and gained bachelor's degrees in both. After graduating, he enrolled for a master's degree in philosophy. It was around this time, his colleagues remember, that his political views began to swing towards the Palestinian cause. Veering wildly across the political spectrum in his search for allegiances, Vanunu had still to discover the religious faith that would enable him to make sense of his life.

A flood of reminiscences reported later in *The Jerusalem Post* illustrate how Vanunu's shifting political beliefs disturbed the people who knew him. No longer the shy student who left no impression on either teachers or fellow students, Vanunu is described as 'latching on' to Arab activists, often arguing their cause 'better than the Arab students themselves'. The ever-present threat posed to Israel by such bellicose Arab leaders as Syria's President Assad and Iraq's President Hussein ensured that Vanunu encountered strong opposition for espousing the Palestinian cause.

One fellow student described him as 'introverted, wily, very intelligent. He was knowledgeable in many fields. He was an ardent opponent of the Government's security policy'. Another said he was 'a real nudnik who tried to fight for his supposed principles, but only spouted rhetoric'.

Balanced against these disapproving reminiscences are those giving a convincing portrayal of Vanunu as a man disturbed by what he saw around him, especially the militarism of the Israeli Government, but not knowing what he could do about it.

Vanunu, as a Moroccan-born Sephardic Jew, was also accused of bitterness towards Israel's Ashkenazi-dominated establishment. (Ashkenazi Jews are those of German and Polish background as opposed to Sephardic Jews, who are those with Spanish, Portuguese or North African backgrounds.)

'He projected a deep sense of deprivation,' Dr Zeev Tsakhor, a history tutor who knew Vanunu at Beersheba, told *The Jerusalem Post*. 'He assumed Ashkenazi dominance in Israel that encompassed all social strata and an Ashkenazi consensus closing off all possibilities of advancement for oriental Jews.'

In time, *The Jerusalem Post*'s reporter declared:

Vanunu's anti-Ashkenazi feelings became anti-Jewish and anti-Israeli. He became the principal spokesman for the Arabs on the Beersheba campus, arguing their case with a growing passion that fellow Jewish students saw assuming an irrational intensity.

Israel's *Ha'aretz* daily reprinted what it said was an interview given by Vanunu in 1985 to a student newspaper at Ben Gurion University. Vanunu was quoted as saying: 'We should stop harassing the Arabs.'

The *Ha'aretz* article linked him with the Communist Party and Israel's left-wing Mapam Party. It also said he had led a campus campaign in support of a lecturer who refused to do military service in Lebanon during the Israeli occupation. *Ha'aretz* said that classmates remembered him as 'weird, and someone who hung out a lot with Arab students'.

Another of his tutors at Ben Gurion, Dr Haim Marantz, offered a less obviously tainted view of Vanunu's Arab sympathies: 'He was concerned to the extent that he took a car to a university on the West Bank and photographed material, the classics in philosophy, for the Arab students in their native language, and that took a bit of guts.'

Dr Marantz was far from being a supporter of Vanunu's subsequent actions—he was later to refuse a request from Vanunu to sign a petition urging the Government to give him an open trial—but his comments assert another side of Vanunu's character that revealed itself at Beersheba: a courage to act forcefully and on his own in support of beliefs that often conflicted dangerously with those of people around him. It was a stark contrast to hearsay reports of his time in the army, where soldiers in Vanunu's sapper unit referred to him slightingly as 'lacking in initiative' and 'shirking responsibility' when he could.

While he was at Ben Gurion, Vanunu considered membership of the Israel Communist Party. Although he attended several meetings of the university group, he was never a card-carrying member. By this time, however, his increasingly visible involvement with left-wing politics, particularly in the cause of Arabs on the West Bank, had come to the attention of Israel's security authorities. Shortly after being photographed at an Arab rally, Vanunu was summoned to an interview with the Shin Bet, Israel's internal security organisation, and senior officials of the Israeli Atomic Energy Authority. As a result of that interview, Vanunu was forced to resign from Dimona in November 1985. The reason given at the time was that Vanunu was one of around 180 employees retrenched in a cost-cutting drive.

What nobody knew was that before he left, Vanunu had photographed the equipment and production processes of Israel's most closely-guarded installation—the top secret nuclear weapons factory known as Machon 2. Eluding random searches and hiding from security guards, Vanunu had roamed beneath false floors built to conceal the bomb factory from international inspectors, shooting two rolls of film on an elderly 35 mm camera he had smuggled into the building in a beach bag. Carrying the exposed films unnoticed past the guards at the gates, he boarded one of the fleet of Volvo buses that passed three times a day through Dimona's electrified perimeter fence. By the time the great dome housing Dimona's central reactor slipped out of sight for the last time, Vanunu was safely in possession of sixty undeveloped colour photographs of equipment, scale models and components used in the manufacture of Israel's nuclear arsenal.

Shortly afterwards, Vanunu sold his car and apartment in Beersheba and left Israel for Europe, Australia and the Far East, telling friends he would never return. Somewhere inside his luggage, undetected by the security checks at Tel Aviv Airport, were two innocuous-looking film canisters.

CHAPTER TWO

DURING THE WEEKS THAT FOLLOWED his first visit to St John's, Vanunu continued going to Operation Nicodemus on Friday and Saturday evenings. Although he had given no hint that he was thinking of becoming a Christian, his dissatisfaction with the Jewish faith and with the Jewish State was already obvious. In the course of their many discussions, David Smith remembers him talking at length about freedom, the fear of freedom, and the Kierkegaardian ideal of making decisions alone and being prepared to take reponsibility for them.

'Kierkegaard has the idea of the individual, and an individual who stands out from the crowd. It is the individual who stands out from the crowd and takes seriously his responsibility before God.'

The willingness to make a momentous decision alone was bound up with Vanunu's understanding of faith as a complete and existential commitment. As David Smith describes it: 'Having the courage to make a decision alone and take responsibility for the things you do was very much part of Mordechai's understanding of Christianity and with the course of action he subsequently took.'

Vanunu earned money by driving a taxi owned by one of the parishioners. He started taking part in regular Bible study groups at St John's. After being given Mark's Gospel, he spent many evenings studying it with David Smith. He did not speak specifically about becoming a Christian, preferring to discuss it abstractly in terms of what it meant to be a Christian and the cost of making such a commitment. He also attended a series of discussion groups organised by Smith. They were entitled 'Following Jesus in a Suffering World' and covered a Christian response to issues such as Third World poverty, racism and nuclear proliferation. It was during one of these meetings that Vanunu revealed that he had worked at Dimona. He said he had some photographs, and suggested showing them to the group as part of a discussion on world peace.

During Bible study classes, Vanunu often criticised Israeli militarism.

As Smith recalls:

> He was strongly opposed to the political values that operated inside Israel. One of the reasons he did not want to go back was that he disagreed with compulsory military service. He spoke about his time working in the arms factory. I don't know whether disgust is too strong a word, but he felt very negative about it and raised the question of doing something about it. He said it was very secretive and he felt what they were doing was wrong. His commitment to peace in a political sense was evident from the start. We talked about that as a Christian duty as well. Even without Christianity, Mordechai was committed to working for peace.

Vanunu was searching for a way to resolve the dilemma of a patriotic duty that contradicted his moral beliefs. As David Smith saw it, his decision to become a Christian was inseparable from his decision to do something about Dimona.

When Mordechai became a Christian I think he knew he would have to act on that. I remember discussing it with him, even when I had no idea of the gravity of the information he had, that perhaps he was in a privileged position to be able to do something in the area of peace which few of us could. I said perhaps it was a God-given opportunity. I believe he took that very seriously, not because I said it, but because he was already committed to peace and then became committed to Christ and the two were always going to be bound up very closely together.

Vanunu was resolved to expose the story of Israel's bomb factory, but it was Oscar Guerrero who gave him the means to do it. Guerrero was a small man, not much bigger than Vanunu, good-looking but a little over-weight, with dark skin and permanently slicked-back hair. He appeared at St John's in June 1986 as part of a government-aided Commonwealth Employment Programme to paint the church fence and hall. He claimed to be a political refugee from Colombia.

McKnight considered painting fences an unlikely occupation for a man like Guerrero, especially as he claimed to be a famous journalist and the confidant of international leaders including the Polish Solidarity leader, Lech Walesa, Cardinal Sin of the Philippines, President Alfonsin of Argentina and the top PLO official Issam Sartawi, who had been assassinated in Portugal in 1983. He also claimed to know the then Israeli Prime Minister, Shimon Peres.

Guerrero backed up his claims with photographs of himself in the company of all these men. McKnight and his colleagues at St John's were easily convinced by the photographs, which showed Guerrero posing stiffly in front of the camera (but never showed him actually talking to anyone else in the picture). They didn't have any reason to doubt Guerrero's claims, or his story that he had been forced to flee Columbia after writing stories critical of the government. McKnight did find it odd that a man like Guerrero should want to earn a living painting church fences, but didn't have any grounds to reject him, so Guerrero got the job, along with two other men, Roland Selicus and William Kinbacher.

In June, Vanunu left his original lodgings at 101 Macleay Street, Kings Cross, and moved into the St John's flats in Darlinghurst Road, opposite the church. He was coming to church regularly and often joined McKnight and other members of staff for morning prayer and breakfast at the rectory.

Guerrero, who had a habit of hanging around the church buildings when he was not working, soon heard about Vanunu's revelations to the study group of his experience at Dimona. Guerrero was not interested in Vanunu's moral dilemma, but he knew a good story when he heard one. The photographs Vanunu had taken inside Dimona, and carried in a rucksack all over Asia, were still not processed. Finally Vanunu went to one of the many photographic processing shops in Darlinghurst Road, where Israel's nuclear secrets spilled out of the machine and piled up among hundreds of tourist snaps of the Sydney Opera House. Vanunu later offered to show the transparencies at one of the parish meetings. McKnight, hearing how dangerous the pictures were, was horrified. Guerrero, too, was horrified, but for rather different reasons.

As soon as Guerrero heard about Dimona he was determined to be involved. Vanunu knew he had to get his story into print, but he didn't know how to do it. Guerrero convinced Vanunu that they had a story which would make both of them rich. Money was not important to Vanunu. He told John McKnight that he would give any money he made from the story to St John's. It was typical of the humility and naivety of a man who said his main ambition in life was to become a server at St John's, passing round the offertory plate. McKnight scorned the idea of giving the money to the parish and warned Vanunu of the dangers he faced from telling the story to the newspapers. He told Vanunu he would need all the money he got to build a new identity for himself.

Money was, and always had been, a side issue for Vanunu, but for Guerrero it was important. Guerrero was a forceful speaker. He pressed Vanunu to let him sell the story through his journalistic contacts. Vanunu, although disturbed by Guerrero's incessant talk of money, and nervous about the dangers of tangling with the Israeli security, knew he would need the Columbian's help to publish the story. Vanunu did not know of Guerrero's reputation for peddling spurious 'scoops', the latest of which involved a photograph of an alleged Indonesian massacre on East Timor, which he tried to sell to *The Sydney Morning Herald* in May 1986. The photograph was recognised as a file picture taken during the Vietnam war, and Guerrero was politely shown the door. But for all Vanunu knew, Oscar Guerrero was who he said he was. He gave Guerrero the outlines of the Dimona story and agreed to hand over some of the photographs for him to show his contacts.

Guerrero's plans then suffered a setback. Part of the project to refurbish the church grounds had included repainting the rectory next door but because of the slowness of the work this was shelved. For some reason they never explained, Guerrero and Roland Selicus, another worker on the CEP scheme, decided to examine the rectory's roof, which was very steep. They didn't say anything to McKnight about it. The route they chose was at the back of the building, via a veranda. They propped one ladder against the veranda, and pulled up another ladder after them, which they rested on the 15 degree slope of the veranda roof. Afterwards, Selicus told McKnight that he climbed up the second ladder onto the rectory roof while Guerrero stood at the bottom and supported the ladder. With nobody else supporting it, Guerrero suddenly started climbing up the ladder.

It was midday and there were few people walking past the church, certainly none who could have walked unnoticed into the rectory grounds. McKnight was sitting inside the rectory in his ground-floor office. He had a full view of the grounds as far as the road. Guerrero was halfway up the veranda roof when the ladder slipped. Still hanging onto the ladder, Guerrero fell down the veranda roof, banged against the veranda wall and fell four metres to the ground. In all, he had fallen about ten metres. McKnight heard the crash and ran outside to find Guerrero lying on the ground while Selicus stared down from the top of the rectory roof. McKnight covered Guerrero with a blanket and dashed inside to call an ambulance, which arrived shortly afterwards and took him to St Vincent's Hospital in Darlinghurst, just a few minutes away.

Guerrero was in hospital for more than a week, suffering mostly from bad bruising. When he came out he had concocted a new story about what had happened on the roof. Guerrero told people he had fallen not ten metres, but fifty—a feat he could only have achieved by leaping off the spire itself. He said a man had deliberately knocked the ladder out from underneath him and that he had spotted a figure running away. Guerrero knew all about the Mossad's reputation for dealing efficiently with its opponents, and insisted it had been a deliberate effort by Israeli agents to kill him. But nobody at St John's had seen this would-be assassin. McKnight saw nothing through the windows of his office. His secretary had seen nothing from her office. In fact, no one had seen anything at all. It would have been impossible for anyone to have dislodged the second ladder without climbing up the first, and Selicus would certainly have seen the culprit if he had had to shimmy down the ladder to make his escape.

Later Guerrero altered his story. A written report of the incident, which St John's had to make out and return to the insurance office in case of an accident claim, made it clear that it was an unauthorised action. A government official came to St John's to photograph the ladder involved in the accident in case there was any evidence of negligence. Guerrero dropped his claims about the Israeli agent and turned his attention to a payout from the church's workers' compensation scheme. The church was found not to have been at fault, and Guerrero's claim lapsed. Years later, his solicitor in Sydney said he was still waiting for Guerrero to contact him from Europe.

By the time he was released from St Vincent's Hospital, Guerrero was ready to tackle Vanunu's story. However dubious his own journalistic credentials, Oscar Guerrero knew his way around the newspaper business, and it didn't take him long to get in touch with journalists in Australia. Late in July, Carl Robinson, the South Pacific correspondent of *Newsweek* magazine, was visited at his home in the suburbs of Sydney by a man calling himself Alberto Bravo and another person identified only as 'David'. They offered *Newsweek* a story which they said proved that Israel had nuclear weapons, but would not tell Robinson where they were staying. They did, however, remain in contact by pay phone, and three weeks later Robinson interviewed 'David' at his home. The interview lasted three hours. Robinson said later that 'David' was so terrified that he had refused, even at the end of the interview, to reveal his real name or to allow Robinson to see his passport or other documents which could prove that he had worked at Dimona. When it was over, Robinson said he needed to check the story through other sources. He asked 'David' to provide more evidence, and said he wanted to see photographs. A week later, 'David' phoned back to say he was too frightened to go ahead with the story. He refused to reveal his real name, but Robinson was later able to identify 'David' as Mordechai Vanunu. 'Alberto Bravo' was a characteristically swaggering pseudonym chosen by Oscar Guerrero.

On 10th August 1986, Mordechai Vanunu was baptised by Stephen Gray at St John's during the morning service. John McKnight led the service, which was attended by 120 friends and members of the parish. He took the baptismal name John Crossman. The ceremony marked the culmination of a search which had taken Vanunu half his life. He wrote later:

> When I came to Sydney I came to the church like I did many times in Europe, but this time I wanted to know more. I came to Sunday morning prayer and I read the New Testament and I found that this was what I was looking for a long time ago, and that my behaviour had a long time before been that of a Christian man. All this means that I had been a Christian for a long time. The spirit of the Lord Jesus was in me.

Though Vanunu had found what he was looking for, he knew the effect his conversion would have on his family. 'My family will hold a funeral for me,' he told David Smith. 'They will consider me dead.'

CHAPTER THREE

GUERRERO FAILED TO INTEREST *The Sydney Morning Herald* in his claims to have the biggest story since Watergate, and so abandoned his efforts to get Vanunu's story published in Australia. Armed with a handful of Vanunu's photographs, he flew to Europe in mid-August, promising to deliver the story to one of his many journalistic contacts there. But Vanunu was now having grave doubts about the whole affair. His moral conviction had not weakened, but he was becoming increasingly nervous of the consequences. Since 1960, when the Mossad had succeeded in kidnapping the Nazi war criminal Adolf Eichmann from Argentina, Israel had made clear its determination to hunt down its enemies in flagrant defiance of international law.

Vanunu knew the dangers he faced by defying the Israeli Official Secrets Act, but they were dangers that did not concern Oscar Guerrero. Making his way to Spain, Guerrero turned up one day at the Madrid office of the London *Sunday Times*. He recounted a dashing tale of a nuclear scientist he had helped smuggle out of Israel with the Mossad in hot pursuit. Guerrero's story finished with the two men escaping to Australia, where they hid in a safe house in Sydney until Guerrero made his dash for Europe.

The Madrid office quickly got in touch with the paper's London headquarters. *The Sunday Times* was interested, but said it would not go any further without meeting Vanunu. Guerrero agreed, and arranged a meeting. He said Vanunu could provide them with all the details they needed. He also told them that Vanunu had two complete rolls of colour film containing pictures of the inner workings of Dimona. *The Sunday Times* assigned one of its top investigative reporters, Peter Hounam, a physics graduate and a senior member of the paper's Insight team, to fly to Sydney to meet Vanunu.

When Hounam got to Sydney he found a different side to Guerrero's story of the disillusioned Israeli nuclear physicist who had been smuggled out of Israel. They met in the Sydney Hilton in the centre of the city. Vanunu explained that he was not a scientist, he was a technician, and he had not been smuggled out of Israel. He corrected the exaggerations in Guerrero's account. Most importantly, he displayed none of the Columbian's gung-ho pursuit of a journalistic scoop. Hounam recalled Vanunu as literally shaking from fright during the first few minutes of the conversation. 'He wasn't sure that I wasn't from the Mossad or the Shin Bet,' he said later.

It was immediately clear to Hounam that the motivation behind Vanunu's action was not money. 'He was prepared to give the information without getting any money.'

Vanunu calmed down after a while, but continued to ask Hounam whether the Dimona story could run without his name on it. But Hounam told him that it was the personal element that gave the story its appeal. Without that nobody would be interested. Hounam also argued that going public with the story would give Vanunu some protection against an attempt by the

Mossad to kidnap him. If nobody knew who he was, nobody could defend him.

Hounam, Vanunu and Guerrero, who was also at the meeting, pulled the curtains of the Hilton hotel room and loaded a box of transparencies into a projector. The film showed dozens of pictures of dials, controls, flow panels and gadgets which Hounam took to be part of the plutonium processing operation at Dimona. Hounam later described his 'gut feeling' that Vanunu was genuine, and that the story before him was a big one.

Peter Hounam spent thirteen more days in Sydney, talking to Vanunu about his life and work, secretly passing the details of Vanunu's photographs back to London for checking. He spent hours in the Mitchell Library in Sydney and put himself through a crash course in nuclear physics and the process of manufacturing atomic bombs. There were people at *The Sunday Times* headquarters in London, he said, who refused to believe Vanunu. It was less than three years since the fiasco surrounding the Hitler diaries, when *The Sunday Times* and a number of respected British historians were deceived by a set of forged diaries, said to have been written by Hitler and now discovered in an East German hayloft. *The Sunday Times*, labelling the story a 'world exclusive', had splashed the find across its front page only to discover that the diaries were fakes. The embarrassing memory of that story was still fresh. *The Sunday Times* could not afford to make a similar mistake with Vanunu.

There were three main questions to verify. First, was the man talking to Hounam really Mordechai Vanunu, and had he worked at Dimona? Second, were the processes shown in the photographs and memorised by Vanunu technically accurate? Last, and most difficult to verify, were these processes actually going on inside Dimona?

Until now, the closest outsiders had managed to get to Dimona was the desert highway running from Beersheba to Sodom. A trickle of blurred photographs taken from speeding cars had found their way into newspaper files around the world, earning a small fortune in reproduction fees for the enterprising photographers. The complex is ringed by an electric fence and the sand inside is regularly raked by tractor to expose footprints to the helicopter and ground patrols. The nearby hilltops bristle with missile batteries ordered to bring down any aircraft straying into the airspace over Dimona. In 1967 an Israeli Mirage III was destroyed when it accidentally overflew the area.

Among the photographs Vanunu had taken were a few external shots of Dimona, and these appeared to tally with what *The Sunday Times* already knew of the complex. In London, information was shown to British government officials without them being told the country involved. British weapons experts contacted by the paper appeared to believe that the information was genuine.

Vanunu had bargained on being able to keep his name out of the story. Anonymity had, from the start, been more important to him than money. As it finally became clear to Vanunu that *The Sunday Times* would not consider running the story of Dimona without bringing him into it, he turned to John McKnight for advice. On 3rd September he confided to him the details of Dimona and the plan to sell his story in London.

McKnight was shown at least twenty photographs. His first reaction was one of disbelief. Working in Kings Cross McKnight met many people and heard many stories. It was not always easy to believe them. But McKnight trusted Vanunu. He overcame his initial scepticism and began to talk to Vanunu about the dangers he would face if he went ahead with his plan. One of the photographs Vanunu showed him was of a flow diagram. McKnight asked if he had thought about the risks of such information getting into the wrong hands and was assured that no information would be released that could be used by terrorists or Israel's enemies. They discussed the possible ramifications of Vanunu's actions and McKnight gave him two letters, one addressed to specific Anglican clergymen he knew in London and the other addressed to any Anglican clergyman asking that should Vanunu present this letter to them then he was in great danger and needed their help. They could ring McKnight reverse charge in Sydney to confirm Vanunu's credentials and McKnight would reimburse them for any out-of-pocket expenses on Vanunu's behalf. He was hoping that the Anglican network would offer at least some refuge if Vanunu ran into danger.

Peter Hounam was getting ready to leave for London with Vanunu. He had been in Sydney for a fortnight and it was time to get Vanunu's photographs, and Vanunu himself, to the scientists and technical experts whose verdict would persuade *The Sunday Times* either to publish or to abandon the story. Besides Vanunu, there were only three people in Sydney who knew the full details of Vanunu's plans: Oscar Guerrero, Peter Hounam and John McKnight. But, as *The Sunday Times* later confirmed, Israel's domestic security agency, the Shin Bet, had already learned about Vanunu's activities several days before the pair flew out of Sydney. A year later Hounam was quoted by *The Jerusalem Post*'s reporter Shalev as saying: 'Another one of the extraordinary things about the Vanunu case, which we know to be a fact, is that four or five days before we flew to London, the Shin Bet knew that Vanunu was in Australia and that he was talking to us.'

What Hounam didn't say was that *The Sunday Times* had inadvertently tipped them off by despatching a reporter to Israel to check up on Vanunu's background.

The Shin Bet, unlike the Mossad, operates only inside Israel and cannot collect intelligence overseas. The only way it could find out about Vanunu's activities in Australia was through its agents in Israel, or through information from one of Israel's foreign embassies. *The Sunday Times* had sent a reporter to Israel around the same time that Peter Hounam left for Australia. The paper wanted to speak to Vanunu's family and friends and discover whatever it could about the Dimona plant from inside Israel. It did not take long for the information to find its way back to Israel and the Shin Bet. Shortly afterwards, Vanunu's family in Beersheba received a visit from Shin Bet agents wanting to know where Vanunu was. The family was told to report any communication they received from him. By the time Peter Hounam was ready to bring Vanunu back to London, both Israel's secret service organisations knew about his intentions. The strenuous efforts made by *The Sunday Times* to prove the truth of Vanunu's story had ensured that Mordechai Vanunu was a marked man long before he touched down at London's Heathrow Airport. The other possible disclosure of Vanunu's plans is contained in allegations that ASIO, the Australian intelligence agency, gave Mossad a file on Vanunu around the beginning of September, and about the same time that Hounam was landing in Sydney.

An incident shortly before the two men left Australia warned Vanunu of the danger he faced in London. Vanunu had arranged, as on many occasions during the fortnight Hounam was in Sydney, to meet and talk at the Hilton Hotel. He was waiting in one of the hotel bars when he became aware of two men talking in Hebrew about Israel. Vanunu was immediately suspicious and, believing the two men to be Mossad agents, hurriedly left the bar and called Hounam down from his room. Hounam came down immediately. He sensed that

Vanunu was nervous but was inclined to believe that the two men were simply Israeli tourists or businessmen. Whether the men really were Mossad agents or whether their innocent conversation sparked something in Vanunu's frightened imagination, the incident served to put both men on their guard.

Vanunu and Hounam flew out of Sydney on 11th September. Vanunu's departure was a sad occasion for his friends at St John's Church in Kings Cross. He had become a well-liked member of the parish and had made a valuable contribution to many of its activities. McKnight, in particular, was worried for his safety in London. The Tarago minibus taking Vanunu to Sydney's Kingsford Smith Airport was nearly full. Vanunu had arranged to meet Peter Hounam at the airport. In the bus with Vanunu were Guerrero, McKnight and several fellow parishioners.

The mood of most of the people in the minibus was tense. Oscar Guerrero, however, was his usual extrovert self, full of the impact he was going to make in London. On the way to the airport he pulled out a fistful of photographs to pass around; they were Vanunu's photographs of Dimona. One person in the vehicle had connections inside the ASIO. Like McKnight, he was alarmed by the plan to publish Israel's nuclear secrets in an English newspaper. He was worried about the potential for such a scheme to deliver the information into the hands of terrorists, and to escalate the dangers of war breaking out in the Middle East. By the time they got out of the bus at the airport, he had decided that it was his duty to inform ASIO about what he had just heard.

Peter Hounam was waiting at the airport, where he hoped that they could meet in safety. When Vanunu walked up to him, Hounam told him that they would no longer be flying by Continental Airlines, as he had previously told him. Hounam had changed the arrangements at the last minute and had booked two seats on a British Airways flight.

When the Tarago minibus pulled up outside St John's church after returning from the airport, one passenger slipped quietly away and phoned ASIO's office in Sydney. He was told to make a full report to the New South Wales police. He went to Darlinghurst Police Station to make his report. At the police station he was told to report the story to a Special Branch officer in College Street, Sydney. He was told that the officer would pass on the details to ASIO.

Speculation over what ASIO did with the information was soon to become acutely embarrassing for the Australian intelligence services. It was standard practice for information concerning Britain to be handed over to MI6. When Hounam and Vanunu landed at Heathrow Airport there were two men from Britain's Special Branch watching them.

CHAPTER FOUR

SINCE THE MID-1950S, ISRAEL'S NUCLEAR AMBITIONS have been nurtured behind twin screens of official secrecy and calculated ambiguity. Hints fed discreetly to a voracious press, and assurances given to concerned allies, were denied in official government announcements the next day. It was a deliberate balancing act which on occasions soured relations with its allies and key arms suppliers, as well exposing Israel to potential pre-emptive attacks by its Arab enemies. But for twenty years this policy allowed the country's leaders to shelter behind the universal assumption that Israel possessed the bomb, while concealing its nuclear technology from all but the inner sanctum of the Cabinet.

Among Israelis, nuclear weapons have long been a non-issue, the confident belief that the country possessed such weapons being reflected in jokes about the 'banana-bending factory' at Dimona.

The history of nuclear power in Israel began almost with the foundation of the state, and grew simultaneously from the country's urgent need to develop agriculture and from its demand for security. With much of its productive land arduously won from the desert, and ready to revert without continuous irrigation, Israel needed a reliable source of water. A nuclear reactor, combined with a desalination plant, would be the source of a regular flow of water which could turn the sand of the Negev Desert into fields to feed Israel's rapidly growing population.

The plan to build such a reactor flourished under the enthusiastic guidance of the country's first Prime Minster, David Ben-Gurion, and the man invited to head the scientific department at the Ministry of Defence, an outstanding former pupil of Albert Einstein called Ernst David Bergmann. The discovery of uranium in the vast phosphate deposits of the Negev Desert ensured a ready supply of fuel for a nuclear reactor. After considering a memorandum completed by Bergmann in July 1954, which canvassed the various nuclear options open to Israel, the Cabinet opted to build a small reactor at Nahal Soreq, on the Mediterranean coast. The decision about a second, larger and more expensive reactor, to be built in the Negev itself, was put off.

The event that forced the Government's hand over Dimona was the Suez crisis of 1956. President Nasser's decision to nationalise the Suez Canal Company in July 1956 brought financial retaliation from Britain, France and the United States and increased tension with Israel. The Egyptians refused to compromise, and Israel invaded on 29th October 1956. Nasser rejected an Anglo-French ultimatum that both Israel and Egypt should halt military operations, and on 29th October Egyptian bases were attacked by French and British planes. This was followed, on 5th November, by an airborne assault on the canal zone. In the course of the fighting, Israeli forces overran both Suez and Gaza, before international pressure forced all three countries to withdraw. The Anglo-French invasion was condemned by the United

Nations, as well as the United States and the Soviet Union. Economic and diplomatic pressure forced an end to the operation, and United Nations' forces were sent in to keep the peace. Nasser enhanced his prestige among the Arabs, while Israel lost confidence in its relationship with the United States. The Government decided that Israel could no longer rely on its former allies to guarantee its security, and had to devise a new strategy for its defence. In 1957 the decision was made to go ahead with the reactor at Dimona. At the same time, Israel took its first steps towards acquiring the bomb. The nation it turned to for help was France.

It was from the start a precarious collaboration, an ostensibly peaceful enterprise whose weapons potential was obvious. It also involved the illicit use of secrets obtained by French scientists during work on the Manhattan Project to produce the atomic bomb that ended the war. The full story of France's co-operation in the Israeli nuclear programme was revealed by Professor Francis Perrin, the former head of France's own bomb project.[1]

According to a report in *The Sunday Times*, Perrin overturned the late President de Gaulle's claim that France had supplied only a peaceful civilian reactor and had denied Israel the technology needed for the manufacture of nuclear weapons.

'In 1957 we agreed to build a reactor and a chemical plant for the production of plutonium,' Perrin said. 'We wanted to help Israel. We knew the plutonium could be used for a bomb, but we considered also that it could be used for peaceful purposes.'

Perrin said that the work had to be secret because of the agreement France had made with the United States over the technical information it had gathered during the development of the bomb in Canada. He said that French scientists involved in wartime work on nuclear weapons had been allowed to continue their work in France only if they kept their Canadian secrets to themselves. The French made the decision to share that information with Israel on the assumption that the Israelis would not let it go any further.

Perrin and de Gaulle agreed at a meeting in 1959 that France should pull out of the joint nuclear weapons programme begun two years before, although construction of the plutonium plant was to go ahead.

Perrin said: 'It was my proposal that we shouldn't be helping Israel build weapons. It was considered that the French military was starting to work too closely with Israel. General de Gaulle stopped the collaboration on nuclear weapons with Israel in 1959, although he agreed to supply the plutonium plant.'

The reasons behind that decision were twofold. De Gaulle was reluctant to renege on France's agreements with Israel. He also saw the benefits for France of working with top Israeli scientists on Dimona. Either way, he decided it was not in France's interest to sever its role in the project. Late in 1960, Shimon Peres flew to Paris for a meeting with the French Foreign Minister, Couve de Murville. At the meeting, Couve de Murville agreed to abandon France's demand for international control over the Israeli reactor.[2] The French companies contracted to supply equipment for the reactor would fulfil their obligations. In return, Ben-Gurion would make a public statement about the reactor and detail the research projects to be conducted there.

Francis Perrin's account of Israel's motive for building the bomb supports the belief that Suez shattered Israeli confidence in its allies.

We thought the Israeli bomb was aimed against the Americans.... Not to launch it against America but to say 'if you don't want to help us in a critical situation we will require you to help us, otherwise we will use our nuclear bombs'.[3]

By 1959, the United States was almost certainly aware of what was going on around Dimona, having detected the first signs of construction from one of its U-2 spy planes in March 1958. This, together with information gained by its agents operating inside Israel, make it unlikely that the Americans could have been deceived for long by the official description of Dimona as a textile factory.

The United States, alarmed by the potentially destabilising effect on the region of an Israeli atomic bomb, and concerned that any future Arab-Israeli war might drag the superpowers into open confrontation, launched two more U-2 flights over Israel in December 1960. The photographs showed that construction of Dimona was far advanced, and there seemed little doubt that the Israelis were planning to build a bomb.

Informed by the CIA that Israel was about to become a nuclear power, President Kennedy sent the US Ambassador, Ogden Reid, to confront the Israeli Government over the issue.[4] On 3rd January 1961, Reid met with Israel's then Foreign Minister, Golda Meir, and presented five questions on behalf of the State Department. He insisted on having his answers by midnight.

The United States wanted to know what would happen to the plutonium produced at the plant and demanded regular inspections of Dimona. Reid demanded an unequivocal statement from Israel that it had no plans to manufacture nuclear weapons.

Ben-Gurion and Golda Meir met and decided not to give their answers by midnight.[5] They waited for the deadline to pass and then summoned the American Ambassador to Sdeh Boker. There Ben-Gurion told him that, as far as Israel knew, plutonium was always returned to the country that supplied the uranium. He refused America's request for international inspections of the plutonium produced in the reactor, declaring that he would not have hostile states meddling in Israel's affairs. He did, however, agree in principle to inspections by its allies or by scientists from an international organisation, but said these could not happen immediately. Ben-Gurion finished by saying that Israel had no plans for any further reactors and had no intention of building nuclear weapons.

In response to pressure from the Americans to come clean over their nuclear objectives, Prime Minister Ben-Gurion had made a statement to the Knesset on 21st December 1960, in which he said: 'With the help of the American Government we have set up a reactor for study purposes in Nahal Rubin with an output of a thousand thermal kilowatts.'

But the issue was not the reactor at Nahal Rubin—which was tiny and posed no conceivable military threat—but the much bigger project at Dimona. It was not until August 1962 that Ben-Gurion made a detailed statement about the Dimona reactor:

> The development of the Negev, which we consider a prime objective for the next decade, necessitates scientific research in many fields. For this purpose we have set up a scientific institute for the study of desert fauna and flora in Beersheba. Also, we are now building a reactor with an output of twenty-four thousand thermal kilowatts for research purposes which will serve the needs of industry, agriculture, medicine and science and prepare Israeli scientific and technical personnel for the construction of a nuclear power station in the future, which we asume will be in ten to fifteen years' time. Like the American reactor, this one too is designed solely for peaceful purposes and has been built under the direction of Israeli experts. It resembles the reactor that the Canadian Government helped install in India, though ours has a smaller output.[6]

Ben-Gurion went on to remind Knesset members that the Foreign Affairs and Security Committee had convened the week before 'to consider the situation created, or likely to come about, as a result of Nasser's demonstration of long-range missiles and the renewed threats against Israel that he made on that occasion'.

The mention of Nasser's threats so soon after his comments about Israel's nuclear research could be taken as at least an acknowledgement that the weapons potential in the 'peaceful' Dimona reactor had not escaped the Government's notice. At most, it could be viewed as part of the scheme of calculated ambiguity—of insisting upon the potential while denying the possession—that has always characterised Israel's nuclear policy.

The military potential inherent in the Dimona project was hotly discussed in the Knesset in 1962, when the Opposition member Yacov Hazan, whose party had twice been in government during the 1950s, said:

> A balance of terror can be maintained only as long as nuclear weapons are restricted to the four Great Powers. The fact that they alone are responsible for their own fate and that of the entire human race is what restrains them and gives humanity hope that a disarmament treaty will be achieved before it is too late. This hope will be reduced to a desperate degree if nuclear arms fall into the hands of numerous other nations, large and small.[7]

The only way out of this dilemma, Hazan insisted, was:

> indefatigable initiative on our part to secure the exclusion from our region of aggressive arms in general and nuclear weapons in particular. Obviously this can be done only if the Great Powers undertake not to provide our region with these weapons or the know-how for their construction and if international supervision is maintained over nuclear development in all countries in the region.

Hazan won the support of the Tewfik Toubi (communists), who said:

The Communist faction in the Knesset calls for a debate in which the Knesset will commit the Government to work for a Middle East free of atomic weapons and remove the danger of these arms being obtained by any government in this part of the world. We may differ on the problem of Palestine and that of relations between Israel and the Arab states. We feel that the Government of Israel is depriving the Palestine Arab nation of its rights and thus placing obstacles in the way of peace. There is no reason why there should not be unanimity in cases where our lives are concerned. The danger of nuclear arms must not be allowed to hang over our heads. We must not permit nuclear weapons to sit in judgment between our two peoples.

The political link between the issues of nuclear disarmament and Palestinian rights had been made in the Knesset well before Vanunu made it.

Prime Minister Ben-Gurion, who five years previously had sanctioned not only the building of the Dimona reactor but also the collaboration with France in the development of nuclear weapons, replied to Yakov Hazan in vague but vigorous fashion:

Knesset member Hazan apparently does not realise that he contradicts himself. He said—and there is a certain amount of truth in it—that the use of atomic weapons anywhere in the world, even by a small country, is liable to lead to a worldwide conflagration. It follows logically that everything should be done to deny access to such arms to any country, large, medium or small. This does not apply to our region alone. For instance, if an atomic bomb is detonated in Patagonia, it will be disastrous; the danger will exist even if there is not one atomic bomb in our entire region.

Ben-Gurion then reminded the Knesset of the Government's policy, which stated that 'until such time as there is general worldwide disarmament, the Government of Israel proposes to all its Arab neighbours —Egypt, Saudi Arabia, Iraq, Jordan, Syria, Lebanon—a treaty for complete disarmament and demobilisation of forces in Israel and the above-mentioned Arab states on condition that constant and free mutual inspection is guaranteed and the sovereign frontiers of each and every one of these states are not infringed.

'Unfortunately,' Ben-Gurion observed, 'our proposal did not receive support from the peace-loving world.'

In late 1963 or early 1964, Ben-Gurion finally allowed US inspectors access to the plant. But elaborate precautions had been taken to ensure that the inspectors would see nothing to compromise the Government's assurances that Dimona was a peaceful project. Workmen had been busy building false walls and bricking up the service elevators to underground floors where work was going ahead on the manufacture of nuclear weapons. The inspectors were kept well away from the most sensitive areas of the plant, and the Dimona scientists so successfully concealed the truth of what they were doing that the inspectors went home convinced that the project was entirely peaceful. After they left, the false walls were quickly pulled down. Six years later, complaining that harassment from Dimona staff made proper investigation impossible, the US abandoned the inspections, allowing the Israeli scientists to carry on their military work undisturbed. Nevertheless, the inspections served a purpose in placating the American conscience, and allowed successive United States Presidents to declare that Dimona was a civilian reactor.

With the inspections over, the work of upgrading and enlarging the twenty-four-megawatt reactor to turn out enough plutonium for Israel's weapons programme progressed unhindered. The essential plutonium reprocessing plant is reckoned to have started up around 1966 or shortly afterwards. This, combined with the weapons expertise provided by the French, left the matter of uranium to power the reactor. Besides the uranium it extracted from its own phosphate deposits, Israel was supplied by Argentina, South Africa and French-controlled mines in Africa.[8] Although these sources gave Israel plenty of fuel to power the initial twenty-four-megawatt reactor, they were not sufficient to power the upgraded reactor needed by Israel for the ambitious weapons-building programme it had embarked upon. To satisfy its expanding need for uranium, Israel had to look for supplies which lay outside the law: first to a uranium processing plant in the United States, and after that to a smuggling operation in Europe.

The first of these did not come to light until two classified documents written in 1976 were made public in November 1977. The memos describing the actions of the National Security Council, the CIA and the FBI were among 3,000 documents released by the Department of Energy under the Freedom of Information Act. They revealed that an inspection made by the US Atomic Energy Commission in 1965 showed up the loss of a large amount of uranium given to the Nuclear Materials and Equipment Corporation (NUMEC) in Pennsylvania to turn into fuel for navy reactors and a space rocket.

Later investigations revealed still greater losses. After analysing waste pits, the AEC concluded that around 390 pounds of uranium had gone missing during the years the plant had been operating. Almost half could be put down as trapped in the machinery, wiping rags and other equipment, which left 200 pounds unaccounted for—enough for between 13 and 20 atomic bombs. Israel was an obvious suspect, given its close links with the company's founder, Zalman Shapiro, a Jewish research chemist who had worked on the Manhattan Project.

The AEC said it was dismayed by the lack of security

and the number of foreign vsitors, notably Israelis, who
had passed through the plant. It found there was a
'highly organised effort on the part of Israel in this
country to solicit substantial technical and financial
assistance' but could not prove that either NUMEC
or Shapiro were agents of Israel. The Carter White
House, worried about harming relations with Jerusalem,
brushed the allegations aside.

In 1967, following the Six Day War—in which Israeli
forces launched a pre-emptive strike against the
Egyptian Air Force and overran the strategically important areas of the Golan, Gaza and the West Bank, as
well as the oil-rich Sinai—a series of international arms
embargoes were imposed against Israel, and France cut
off the flow of uranium to Dimona.

According to an article in *Rolling Stone* magazine, it
was left to the Mossad to conjure up a new supply.[9] A
specially created commando unit made four uranium
hijackings in Europe, two with the co-operation of
France and West Germany. The Mossad allegedly
grabbed low-grade uranium in England that had been
wrongly labelled as enriched or bomb-grade. A statement from the chairman of the House interior and
insular affairs committee, Senator Morris Udall,
appeared to substantiate the *Rolling Stone* allegations.
A spokesman for British Nuclear Fuels Ltd described
the story as 'absolute nonsense' and the Atomic Energy
Authority issued a similar denial. A spokesman for the
Israeli Embassy in Washington declared: 'The Israelis
have never hijacked any enriched uranium either in the
United States or anywhere else in the world.' In New
York, the Israeli Consul-General reverted to an old
refrain: 'Israel will not be the first to introduce nuclear
weapons to the Middle East.' Like previous efforts to
prise open Israel's nuclear secrets, the story settled into
stalemate.

In 1968 the Mossad achieved their most spectacular success—the hijacking of 200 tons of Belgian uranium from a ship in the Mediterranean.[10] Discovery of the sophisticated operation came about five years later as the result of a freak incident in Norway and some uncharacteristic bungling on the part of the Mossad. Norwegian police arrested a Mossad agent after a botched assassination attempt on a senior Palestinian official thought by the Israelis to have been involved in the massacre of Israeli athletes at the Munich Olympics. The mission turned into a disaster for the Mossad hit squad after they accidentally gunned down an innocent waiter in Lillehammer and managed to get themselves arrested by the local police. One member of the squad, Dan Aerbel, who had been involved in the operation, was overcome by claustrophobia after a night in the cells and blurted out an extraordinary story to his bewildered captors. Norwegian counter-intelligence was called in to interrogate the captured agent, and by the time Aerbel had finished, he had blown the lid off a story that the European Commission and Euratom had managed to cover up for five years. He revealed how a Belgian uranium shipment bound for a fake address in Milan—where it was to be processed into a catalyst for use in the petrochemical industry—had been inter-cepted in the Mediterranean and transferred, in barrels marked 'plumbat' (based on the Latin word for lead), into a heavily escorted Israeli merchant ship. The empty ship, the 'Scheersberg A', was owned by Dan Aerbel.

Euratom, the European nuclear regulatory agency, discovered the loss, but it was powerless to obtain answers from the Israelis or from the Italian company, SAICA, the varnish producer which was supposed to process the uranium for the Israeli petrochemical industry. When the 'Scheersberg A' was finally tracked down by West German investigators, the relevant pages

44

of the ship's log had been ripped out. The European Commission, knowing that its own regulations had been breached when the sensitive uranium cargo left European waters without a special export licence, hoped that by closing the file they would be able to keep the whole affair secret. The Israelis and the sympathisers acting for them in Europe were certainly in no hurry to say anything. If it hadn't been for the Mossad's bungled assassination attempt in Lillehammer, the 'Plumbat affair' might never have been discovered.

By 1973, Israel's nuclear industry had no need for such hazardous operations to secure materials for its weapons programme. In 1970, Isaiah Nebenzahl, a physicist with the Ministry of Defence, and Menahem Levin, from Tel Aviv University, pioneered a sophisticated technique of extracting uranium-235 from ordinary uranium by bombarding it with laser beams. It was a process which had been tried without success by research teams in the United States looking for cheaper methods of producing enriched uranium. American reactions to the Israeli team's breakthrough were varied. Robert Gillette, of *Science* magazine, commented that the reaction among US scientists was one of 'astonishment tinged with disbelief' and concluded that 'the Israelis are building bombs in their basements'. Richard Levy, head of a US company engaged in laser enrichment research, hoped that the reports weren't true, but added, 'It's a peculiar way to announce a nuclear weapons programme ... it shook a lot of us up.'[11]

Having secured the expertise and the uranium, only one more ingedient was needed by Israeli scientists to get their nuclear weapons programme underway: heavy water.

Heavy water looks like ordinary water but is rich in deuterium, a heavy isotope of hydrogen. Its value in the atomic process is that it slows down neutrons passing through it. At lower speeds fission occurs between the neutrons and the unstable uranium isotope U-235. Fission releases energy and more neutrons fly off, setting off a chain reaction. Heavy water slows down the neutrons without absorbing them, and is essential for reactions using natural uranium, which contains only 0.7 per cent U-235.

Ordinary water can also be used in starting a chain reaction, but enriched uranium is needed in order to offset its greater absorbtion of neutrons. This normally means boosting the proportion of U-235 to about 3 per cent, a difficult and expensive process needing sophisticated technology and vast amounts of electricity. Smuggling operations had given Israel a useful supply of the enriched material, but it was not enough to service the country's weapons programme. Lacking the techniques to manufacture its own, Israel had to get hold of enough heavy water to operate its nuclear reactor with natural uranium instead. The plutonium needed to build a bomb would be extracted from the used fuel rods. As Professor Gary Milhollin, a US expert in the transfer of nuclear technology, writes: 'Heavy water is the cheaper way to the bomb.... Because of heavy water, France, India and Israel all have been able to make nuclear explosives free of international control.'[12]

According to Milhollin, in the early 1960s only Norway and the United States had any heavy water for export, and both restricted exports to peaceful use. Israel hed developed the technology to produce small amounts for itself, but not enough. It was committed to importing heavy water, and that could only come from the United States or Norway. The only other route—via France—would have meant illegally diverting stocks which must have originated in one of those two countries.

The United States sent 3.9 tonnes directly to Israel in 1963, three years after its U-2 spy planes had picked up decisive evidence of what was happening at Dimona. According to officials of the International Atomic Energy Authority, which is based in Vienna and has more than 100 member states, Israel insisted that it was for peaceful use and pledged to keep it under international inspection.[13] The IAEA contends that the heavy water is still in Israel and is still under IAEA supervision, but admits that heavy water stocks were barely looked at until the late 1970s. So Israel alone knows what happened to it in the interim.

The other confirmed source of heavy water for Dimona was a shipment of 20 tonnes from Norway, which was approved at the last minute and delivered in 1959. Milhollin insists that Israel could not have counted on the Norwegian shipment and must therefore have obtained enough heavy water to get started from France, which supplied the reactor. He also says that the total amount of heavy water Israel received from the three sources points to a reactor considerably bigger than the one Israel admits to having. Assessments of the size of the reactor, based on Prime Minister Ben-Gurion's speech to the Knesset, have traditionally ranged from twenty-four to twenty-six megawatts, Milhollin suggests the reactor would need to have been boosted to more that 100 megawatts to require that amount of heavy water. Milhollin's estimate is broadly consistent with reports that began to appear in the early 1980s indicating that the original reactor had been enlarged to as much as three times its original size, and that this had taken place some time after the final US inspection in 1969. Further evidence that the original capacity of the reactor had been dramatically boosted came from Vanunu himself, and centred on the rate of plutonium production at Dimona, which was many times what would have been possible with a twenty-four megawatt reactor.

The questions surrounding Norway's original heavy water shipment have still not been answered. According to Milhollin:

Norway's Foreign Ministry says that Israel made three pledges when it imported the 20 tonnes in 1959: to restrict the water to peaceful use, to re-transfer it only with permission, and to allow inspection of any facility where it was used. These pledges would cover any plutonium made by a reactor using the heavy water. The agreement was secret when made, but Norway released the details in October 1986. Israel imported an additional one tonne in 1970 under the same restrictions.

In February 1987, prompted by questions in Parliament and newspaper reports that Norway had not enforced its rights, the Norwegians asked Israel to let the IAEA inspect the heavy water. Such an inspection would be able to ascertain whether the heavy water had been used in a reactor. If it had, then Israel would be obliged to allow the plutonium produced in the reaction to be checked to ensure it honoured the peaceful-use pledge. Norway's only inspection had been in 1961, two years before Dimona was started.

In April 1987, Israel, disputing neither its receipt of the water nor the pledges it had made, declared that it could not trust the IAEA to be objective. Norway made a formal demand for international inspection on 30th September, 1987. Israel flatly refused.

The heavy water controversy blew up again in May 1988, when the possibility was raised that two more shipments of Norwegian heavy water may have been illegally diverted from their intended destinations. One involved fifteen tonnes of heavy water intended for West Germany but diverted to the international black market. The other concerned a twelve and a half tonne shipment of heavy water exported to Romania in 1986 which Norwegian officials suspected may have been sent to another country by the Romanians. India, whose nuclear reactors are not under international safeguards, was suggested as a possible destination for illegally diverted heavy water. So was Israel.

In June 1988, the dispute between Israel and Norway was finally settled when Israel agreed to allow inspections of the heavy water remaining from the original shipment. But by now the original aim of the inspections had been abandoned. Norwegian officials said that Norway would not, after all, be able to determine whether Israel had used the heavy water for nuclear weapons. Israel had proved that the guardians of nuclear power were impotent.

Furthermore, it had taken for itself the role of guardian over the nuclear aspirations of its Arab neighbours, a role it has secured with little effective opposition from the great powers, despite the dangers that its pre-emptive actions pose in such a volatile region. On 7th June 1981, Israeli jets destroyed Iraq's Osiraq nuclear reactor near Baghdad. Built by the Soviets in 1963, the reactor had troubled the Israelis since 1975, when France and Iraq completed a nuclear co-operation agreement exchanging French nuclear aid for oil. Commentators were quick to see the dangers of Israel's nuclear one-upmanship.

Like a bolt out of the Old Testament, they hurtled at Baghdad out of the setting sun. Nearing their target, six F-15 interceptors camouflaged with the desert mottle of the Israeli air force peeled off to keep guard overhead. Eight F-16 fighter-bombers roared down on the concrete dome of the Osiraq nuclear reactor. In a single series of lightning passes, the little fighters dropped their payload of 2,000 lb bombs. Within two minutes they disappeared cleanly into

the gathering darkness, leaving behind a few puffs of flak—
and a fearsome new turn in a dangerous nuclear game.[14]

Israel's then Prime Minister, Menachem Begin,
described the raid as an act of self-defence and claimed
that he had concrete proof that Iraq was planning to use
the reactor to build nuclear weapons which it would use
against Israel. Begin branded Iraq's Saddam Hussein a
meshugeneh (madman) intent on Israel's nuclear
destruction. He said Israel had no choice but to attack
immediately, claiming that the Iraqi reactor was to be
loaded with highly enriched uranium as early as 1st
July, and that the radioactive fallout of any later raid
might have devastated Baghdad. Israel's vulnerability
and its martyred past had made the strike Israel's right,
he insisted, and his duty. 'There will never be another
Holocaust in the history of the Jewish people,' Begin
said. 'Never again, never again.'

The raid attracted strong criticism, especially from
the Soviet Union, the Arab countries and western
Europe, but this was short-lived. Reaction in the United
States was on the whole more cautious but included a
memorable tirade from Senator Mark Hatfield, a
Republican moderate from Oregon, who condemned
Israel's 'enormous and dangerous arrogance' and
described the Israeli attack as 'one of the most pro-
vocative, ill-timed and internationally illegal actions
taken in that nation's history'.

The planes used in the raid were F-16s supplied by
the United States. The White House, ambiguously condemning the raid for its 'unprecedented character', and
clearly annoyed by the use of US planes in the raid,
initially declared that it would withhold the planned
delivery of four F-16s, and would consider stopping a
shipment of six more. Shortly afterwards, it announced
that the delivery of all ten planes would go ahead after
all. Iraq, meanwhile, took the opportunity to build

bridges with the United States, and collaborated with the United States on working out a 'compromise' ruling in the United Nations Security Council. Resolution number 487 condemned Israel's action but stopped short of imposing sanctions. The United States was saved from having to use its veto. The Soviet Union was not accommodated in the US/Iraqi deal, but the international crisis looming in the days following the raid had been averted.

Tepid opposition at home was swamped by the euphoria of a spectacularly successful mission, ably assisted by Prime Minister Begin's invocation of the Holocaust and his promise that Israel would defend itself with any means at its disposal. The Israeli Labour Party's claim that the raid was electorally inspired seemed more than plausible in the light of the 82.9% public approval recorded on the eve of the elections.[15] The raid plainly did no harm to Begin's Likud Government, which overturned Labour's early gains and was able to form another Government with the support of three minor parties. Israel had added a new dimension to its vow not to introduce nuclear weapons into the region, by proving its determination to stop anybody else not introducing them first.

CHAPTER FIVE

ISRAEL'S CAPACITY TO BUILD THE BOMB had never been doubted, but proof that it already possessed one was hard to obtain. In May 1969, the German magazine *Der Spiegel* produced a story claiming that the Israelis had built five bombs and had almost finished a sixth. The story broke several days before the magazine went to press, when the *Montreal Gazette* reported the story on its front page. The newspaper's German affairs correspondent wrote:

'Last January, the National Broadcasting Company aired a program alleging that Israel's first nuclear bomb was almost ready. Israel issued an immediate denial.

'It appears, however, that NBC missed the exact date by only 18 days. The bombs were completed during early February.'

The report went on to say that Egyptian intelligence had become aware of the completion of the bombs in late February, prompting President Nasser to request the Soviet Union to station nuclear arms on its soil.

'Moscow refused,' the report said, 'but strengthened the Soviet Mediterranean fleet to include ships equipped with nuclear warheads.'

It claimed that Israel could deliver nuclear bombs with its A-8 Skyhawk jets.

The Israeli press featured the Montreal report prominently, but without comment, while the Israeli Foreign Ministry spokesman dismissed the claims as 'speculative, inaccurate and unauthoritative', adding that Israel 'is not an atomic power'.[16]

Der Spiegel later insisted that most of the information in the article had been obtained first-hand.

In 1970, a new element was added to the already flexible Israeli formula of not being the first country to introduce nuclear weapons to the Middle East. This was the so-called 'last-wire issue'—whether Israel should be judged to have an atomic weapon before the last wire or piece of mechanism is hooked up.

The New York Times declared that Israel either had the bomb, or had the components to make one. It said in a front-page report that both former President Lyndon Johnson and then President Nixon had received intelligence reports 'that Israel has the capacity to assemble an atomic bomb and that some senior officials believe that she has already done so'.

The report claimed there had been disagreement among senior US Government officials over whether the evidence was conclusive. 'As long ago as 1968 the White House had no doubt that Israel could produce an atomic bomb or warhead for her French-built surface missiles and that if such a weapon was not already in being, it was within very easy range.'

It quoted highly placed sources as saying that Richard Helms, the director of the Central Intelligence Agency, told the Senate Foreign Relations Committee at a closed-door hearing on 7th July 1970: 'The American estimate was that Israel has the technical capacity to make atomic weapons.'

In March 1976, the CIA hosted a cocktail party in

Washington for 150 members of the American Institute of Aeronautics and Astronautics. The invitation had promised an 'unclassified briefing' to the guests on the intelligence work of the CIA in its pursuit of a peaceful world. As well as the cocktails, the CIA promised a question-and-answer session hosted by Carl Duckett, the deputy director for Science and Technology and the CIA's top technical analyst. In a moment of reckless candour, Duckett let slip the CIA's belief that Israel had 'ten to twenty' nuclear weapons 'available for use'. Duckett added that he would not like to see the estimate quoted in the newspapers. When the remark turned up in the *Washington Post* dated 15th March, 1976, Duckett's boss, the CIA's then director, now President George Bush, apologised for Duckett's indiscretion and called it 'unfortunate'. Bush did not deny its accuracy.

One of the most startling accounts of Israel's nuclear arsenal came to light as the result of a bureaucratic error by the CIA. It concerned a CIA report entitled 'Prospects for Further Proliferation of Nuclear Weapons', written in 1974, soon after India exploded a nuclear device. The report was stamped 'SECRET: NO FOREIGN DISCLOSURE', but the text was mistakenly released in January 1978 under a suit filed by the National Resources Defence Council. It was the first time the CIA had put its opinions about Israel's nuclear weapons capacity in the public record. The five-page document stated catagorically that Israel was building nuclear weapons. The report, all but two paragraphs of which should have remained classified, said:

> We believe that Israel already has produced nuclear weapons. Our judgement is based on Israeli acquisition of large quantities of uranium, partly by clandestine means, the ambiguous nature of Israeli efforts in the field of uranium enrichment, and Israel's large investment in a costly missile system designed to accommodate nuclear warheads.

The report concluded: 'We do not expect the Israelis to provide confirmation of widespread suspicions of their capability, either by nuclear testing or by threat of use, short of a grave threat to the nation's existence.'[17]

In fact, the 'grave threat to the nation's existence' which the CIA believed could provoke Israel into showing its nuclear hand had already occurred, during the near-disaster of the 1973 Yom Kippur War.[18]

After forty-eight hours of fighting, the Egyptians had beaten off the first Israeli counter-attacks along the Suez Canal, causing heavy casualties, and Israeli forces on the Golan Heights were retreating in front of a fierce Syrian tank assault. At 10 pm on 8th October, the Israeli commander on the northern front, Major General Yitzhak Hoffi, warned his chief of staff: 'I am not sure we can hold out much longer.' The message was passed to Moshe Dayan, at that time Israel's Defence Minister. Shortly after midnight, Dayan went to see Prime Minister Golda Meir. Dayan told the Prime Minister: 'This is the end of the Third Temple,' an allusion to the temples in Jerusalem destroyed by invading Babylonians in 586 BC and by the Romans in AD 70. Mrs Meir gave permission for Israel's stockpile of nuclear weapons to be assembled. In a matter of hours scientists put together thirteen nuclear bombs in a secret underground tunnel and rushed them to waiting Phantoms and Israeli-built Kfir fighters. But before the bombs were primed, the battles for Suez and the Golan had turned in Israel's favour. The bombs were dismantled and hidden away in underground bunkers in the Negev.

The whole operation had been spotted by the Soviets, probably from their Cosmos spy satellite over the Middle East. On 13th October, the Soviets loaded a ship with nuclear warheads capable of being fitted to the Scud missiles based in Egypt. The Americans picked up the ship as it passed through the Bosphorus, on its way from the naval base at Nikolayev to Alexandria. The news was immediately passed to Washington, and the Americans issued a world military alert. The United States was effectively preparing for war. The Soviets, only one step away from arming a nuclear client in the middle of a war zone, backed off.

Throughout the late 1970s and early 1980s, a trickle of mostly unsubstantiated reports raised the possibility that Israel might possess many more than the 'ten to twenty' nuclear weapons suggested by the CIA, but it was not until 1985 that the idea of an arsenal comprising some hundreds of weapons began to appear in the press. In May 1985, two reports in the respected *Aerospace Daily*, citing unnamed 'US sources', stated that Israel might possess as many as 200 nuclear weapons and that since 1981 it had deployed nuclear-armed Jericho II missiles, with a range of 400 miles. The reports described the Jericho II as a solid-fuel rocket developed in the mid to late 1970s, with a new and far more accurate guidance system than its predecessor, the Jericho I.

The author of the reports, Richard Sale, provided more information during a television interview on the NBC's *Nightly News* programme in July 1985. Sale named the Weizman Institute near Tel Aviv as the place where the warhead was developed, and said that US scientists had been involved in the project. Sale gave a detailed description of the warhead, which he said came from an American scientist who had seen it. In an interview with Leonard Spector, mentioned in Spector's book *Going Nuclear*, Sale claimed that his reports had been confirmed by several official and private sources in the United States who were familiar with Israeli military programmes.[19]

Another Middle East expert, Anthony Cordesman, who appeared with Sale on the NBC broadcast, claimed that Israel had at least 100 nuclear weapons, and possibly more than 140.

The one item missing from the Israeli nuclear equation—and the one that sustained Israel's pretence of not being a nuclear power—was that the country had never been known to test a nuclear device. This by itself was not an obstacle to possessing an active weapon. The Swedes, in their nuclear research programme in the late 1950s, had designed and tested the components of atomic weapons weighing 600 kilograms—a size comparable with the warhead on Israel's Jericho II missile—without conducting a full-scale nuclear test. The Swedes were confident about their ability to build the bomb without the need to explode it.[20] The Israelis, it was believed, would be able to do the same.

Without the proof of a nuclear test, Israel continued to debunk the mainly circumstantial evidence that it had the bomb. But in 1980, new evidence came to light suggesting that Israel had finally exploded a nuclear device. This time help came not from France, but from a country with nuclear ambitions of its own and little to lose by flouting the non-proliferation treaty it had refused to sign. With its enormous uranium resources, vast territory and high technological base—including an incipient uranium enrichment industry—South Africa was an invaluable partner.

During the 1950s, when the peaceful use of atomic energy was vigorously promoted, Israel and South Africa both benefited from US-sponsored atomic energy programmes. South Africa was able to trade uranium for nuclear technology from the United States, as well as from Britain, France and West Germany. But increasing international opposition to apartheid, and South Africa's refusal, like Israel, to sign the Nuclear Non-proliferation Treaty, meant that the flow of technology and information gradually dried up. The flourishing arms trade between Israel and South Africa made them natural allies in the search for the bomb.

In 1965, after South Africa's Safari I reactor came on line, Israeli scientists began helping South Africa with its Safari II research reactor. A novelised account of Israel's nuclear programme, banned by the Israeli censor before it could be published, indicates that South Africa first suggested testing Israeli nuclear weapons in its territory as early as 1966. Israel turned down the offer. The authors of the novel, the Israeli journalists Eli Teicher and Ami Dor-on, outsmarted the censor by giving a detailed interview to an American correspondent, Dan Raviv, who then broadcast the story from Rome.

The authors, whose sources included Shimon Peres, a key political figure in the development of the Israeli bomb, alleged that the South African Prime Minister, John Vorster, again offered the Israelis a nuclear test site during a visit to Israel in April 1976. The following year, a Soviet satellite picked up unmistakable signs of preparation for a nuclear test in the Kalahari Desert. On 6th August, 1977, the information was passed to the Carter administration and to the three major European powers. Fearing that the test would trigger a dangerous new escalation in the nuclear arms race, the United States, Britain, France and West Germany joined forces with the USSR to stop the test. Officials in Washington were convinced that the device to have been exploded was Israeli.

In 1979, an explosion was observed at a spot on the edge of the South Atlantic and Indian oceans in an area known as the 'South African anomaly', where the radiation belts circling the earth drop to sea level.

A US Vela spy satellite hovering over the area recorded the double flash of light characteristic of nuclear explosions. It was a small blast, carried out in an area of high natural radioactivity. It was designed to leave very little evidence. The CIA told the National Security Council that a two or three kiloton bomb had been exploded in what it called a 'joint South African-Israeli test'. A US Navy official later revealed that US spy planes over the test area had been waved away by South African Navy ships and forced to land secretly in Australia. Through its extensive spy network inside South Africa, the CIA knew about the fleet of specialised ships which had left the port of Simonstown in early September. Although it did not know the purpose of the mission, the CIA knew that South African ships were conducting secret manoeuvres at the site of the test. In Washington, the South African military attaché made an unprecedented request to the US National Technical Information Service for a computer search on detection of nuclear explosions and orbits of the Vela satellite.[21]

The Carter Administration convened a special panel to investigate the incident. The US Naval Research Laboratory, the Defense Intelligence Agency and the CIA, and representatives of the Los Alamos National Laboratory, the Department of Energy and the State Department presented evidence to the inquiry supporting the occurrence of a nuclear explosion, possibly of a neutron bomb. A month after the incident, the State Department issued a carefully worded statement in which it announced that:

> The US Government has an indication suggesting the possibility that a low-yield nuclear explosion occurred on September 22 in an area of the Indian Ocean and South Atlantic ... No corroborating evidence has been received to date. We are continuing to assess whether such an event took place.[22]

As the CIA and numerous defence experts became convinced that a nuclear test had taken place, the

Carter White House backed off. New information was ignored by the panel. Signs of radiation discovered in the thyroid glands of Australian sheep was discounted. In direct contradiction of the State Department's original statement, press reports in February 1980 quoted Carter Administration officials as saying there was 'no evidence' that the signal picked up by a US satellite was the flash from an atomic test. The White House position was backed up by irate denials from the Israeli and South African Governments. The then Israeli Defence Minister, Ezer Weizmann, was quoted on Israel Radio as saying there was 'no truth or foundation in the report'. The South African Foreign Minister, Pik Botha, announced: 'I know absolutely nothing about the matter—why don't you ask the Russians or the Chinese, or even the Americans for that matter?' Botha said that the claimed area of the detonation made the allegations ridiculous, and wryly suggested that 'we might even be talking about Australia or New Zealand'.

The US panel focused excitedly on the possibility of a 'zoo event', a piece of scientific jargon meaning that something inexplicable had happened. Seven months after President Carter had initiated the investigation, the White House panel declared that the signal received by the Vela satellite was probably caused by the impact of a small meteorite, a verdict upheld by the Reagan Administration in May 1985.

The ramifications of acknowledging that a nuclear test had taken place might have wrecked the Camp David accords between Israel and Egypt, and upset negotiations over the creation of Zimbabwe, in which South African co-operation was needed.

For the United States, acknowledging the truth about Israel's nuclear weapons remained diplomatically impossible, as a State Department official explained to *Inquiry* magazine: '[It] would be a major turning point in our relations with South Africa and Israel if we determined conclusively that either had tested a nuclear bomb. It makes me terribly nervous just to think about it.'[23]

The United States accepted the damage to its already tarnished non-proliferation policy and, like the servicemen it had sent to observe US nuclear tests in the Pacific, turned its back on the matter.

CHAPTER SIX

IN THE THIRTY-SEVEN YEARS SINCE ITS FORMATION, the Mossad has run up a list of spectacular successes. The Eichmann kidnapping, a spate of political assassinations and the repatriation of five missile boats embargoed by the French in Cherbourg harbour left no doubt about its ability to deal with a single troublemaker walking alone in the streets of London. Unwittingly forewarned by *The Sunday Times* of Vanunu's intention to reveal its atomic secrets to the world, but unable to stifle him, the Israeli Government was certain to assign the Mossad to bring the so-called traitor to justice. The question was when—and how?

Yitzhak Shamir, who was about to take over as Prime Minister from Shimon Peres under a rotation agreement, was reported to have wanted Vanunu assassinated while he was still in Australia.[24] According to Louis Toscano, the former Jerusalem bureau chief of United Press International, the hardliner Shamir insisted that Vanunu was a traitor, and there was only one way to deal with such a man. Peres believed Vanunu's revelations would send a sobering signal to the Arabs, particularly Syria and Iraq, and ruled against it, supported by the Defence Minister, Yitzhak Rabin. Peres dismissed the assassination claim as 'cheap gossip'.

By the time he reached London in September 1986, Vanunu was acutely aware of the dangers he faced, and was relying on the promise made to him by *The Sunday Times* to provide him with a new identity in return for his co-operation. Vanunu had agreed to fly to London in the belief that he would only be needed for two weeks. He believed that such a brief stay would give the Mossad no time to plan and execute an operation to get him back to Israel. Once he was back in Australia, he thought he would be safe.

But *The Sunday Times*, while at pains to protect the source of the story that had fallen into its lap, could only look after Vanunu as far as he would let them. Vanunu was independent, a wanderer who had spent much of the past year backpacking through Asia. He was also impatient, and frightened. Vanunu resented being dependent on others for his safety, and was not prepared to risk the lives of other people if the abduction he feared did take place. Vanunu was under no illusions about the dangers he faced from the Mossad, but was just naive enough to think that he could outwit them. McKnight comments:

> He knew that he could be kidnapped or killed. We talked about it often. I think he even half-believed that he would die for what he was doing, but was prepared to go through with it anyway for the sake of peace and his commitment to nuclear disarmament. But Mordi always said that he would be coming back to Australia very soon. He spoke about it as a short trip. Mordi told everyone he would be safe in Australia by the time the story came out in London.

The Sunday Times made a determined effort to keep Vanunu's whereabouts secret, and assigned a succession of reporters to keep an eye on him. For three weeks, Vanunu was moved around London from one safe house to another. For a while he stayed under a false name at a country hotel in Welwyn about fifty kilometres outside London, where nobody knew his business and even the proprietor knew nothing about his real identity. During this time, Vanunu was exhaustively questioned by *Sunday Times* reporters. The ease with which *The Sunday Times* had got hold of the story, and Vanunu's almost incredible feat in photographing the inner workings of Dimona, left a suspicion that the whole story could be a plant by the Mossad designed to intimidate Israel's Arab neighbours.

The Sunday Times called in some of Britain's leading nuclear experts, including Dr Frank Barnaby, with the aim of exposing the flaws in Vanunu's account. He was challenged on subjects he ought to know and on subjects that were far outside the likely knowledge of a technician. Vanunu satisfied the experts on both counts. He knew as much as he claimed but no more.

The deal Vanunu had made with *The Sunday Times* promised him $US 75,000 in return for the exclusive rights to the story and the pictures, and the rights for a book. Vanunu said he wanted the first $US 25,000 to go to Guerrero. The part of the deal concerning Guerrero was confirmed in a letter dated 11th September 1986, and signed on behalf of *The Sunday Times* by Peter Hounam the same day he left Australia with Vanunu. The typed letter was headed 'Re: Oscar Edmundo Guerrero' and said:

This is to confirm arrangements for the payment of a fee for introducing this newspaper to Mr Mordechai Vanunu and arranging interviews with Mr Vanunu for his story of his experiences working for the Israeli Atomic Energy Commission. We agree that from the first monies paid to Mr Vanunu on publication of his story *The Sunday Times* shall deduct a total of $25,000 (US) and pay this to Mr Guerrero. We shall ensure that in finalising (sic) the contract with Mr Vanunu this commitment is recognised.

At the bottom of the page is a handwritten note: 'Money to be paid into Mr Guerrero's bank in Sydney, Australia. ... Paid cash today A$ 500.'

The document was not enough to convince Oscar Guerrero that his money was safe.

In London, verification of the story took much longer than Vanunu expected, and he grew increasingly demoralised as the paper insisted on checking and rechecking every detail. The longer it went on the more worried Vanunu became that the paper was losing interest, and the more frightened he became for his own safety.

Since arriving in England, Vanunu had rung John McKnight in Sydney every five or six days. At first the calls were confined mainly to the concerts Vanunu had heard, the churches he had visited, and the galleries he had seen. Quite suddenly the tone of the calls changed. Vanunu began to sound tense and impatient. It wasn't hard to discover the reason—Oscar Guerrero had surfaced in London.

Guerrero was afraid that he was being elbowed out of the deal. He had been to see McKnight a few days after Vanunu left. He told McKnight he was going to London. He insisted that the whole story was his idea, that he had been the one to make contact, and that without him the story would never have got off the ground. The way Guerrero told it, Vanunu's own role seemed incidental.

Guerrero was suspicious of everyone. He showed McKnight the typed letter from *The Sunday Times* confirming his share of the deal. The letter didn't stop him feeling he was being left out. He said he was flying to London to protect his stake. McKnight didn't attempt to talk him out of making the trip, but he did wonder how Guerrero could afford it. Guerrero said *The Sunday Times* had paid for his ticket but he needed some money to live on. McKnight sensed the way the conversation was drifting and guessed that Guerrero was going to ask him for money. Guerrero did, and McKnight refused.

Oscar Guerrero was the last man Vanunu wanted running loose in London. *The Sunday Times* had convinced Vanunu that the Columbian could not be trusted. They analysed some of the photographs Guerrero had been passing around, showing him talking to international leaders. They concluded that several of the photographs were fakes, but very high quality ones—not the sort of thing that could be done in a bathroom.

When Vanunu found that Guerrero was in London he rang McKnight in Sydney and asked him not tell Guerrero anything—not to let him know where he was staying and not to say anything that would enable him to find out.

At the same time he told McKnight that *The Sunday Times* was being cautious about publishing the story. He knew that the longer they delayed the more danger he was in. McKnight found him anxious, but still determined to get the story published.

Vanunu was restless and frustrated and bored. He decided to leave the safety of his country hotel and told *The Sunday Times* he wanted to move back to London. It suited *The Sunday Times* to have him closer to the paper's headquarters, but they were worried about being able to protect him in the city. Vanunu, however, felt that the city crowds were his best protection. Vanunu came back to London and booked in at the Mountbatten Hotel in Covent Garden under the name Mr George Forsty. Although his address was known to only a handful of people at *The Sunday Times*, Vanunu's movements were by now being closely watched by the Mossad, whose agents could latch onto him unnoticed in the mêlée of union pickets and police outside News International's besieged Wapping headquarters.

By late September, Vanunu had been thoroughly

debriefed by *The Sunday Times*. On 23rd September, the Israeli Embassy in London was formally approached for comment, and presented with a summary of the technical detail gathered by the paper, together with Vanunu's story and photographs, a copy of his passport and the scientific assessment carried out by Dr Frank Barnaby and other experts. The embassy initially brushed the story aside, saying that such stories were commonplace and entirely untrue and did not merit any further comment. An invitation by *The Sunday Times* to the authorities in Tel Aviv to supply evidence proving the story to be a hoax resulted, after some hours' deliberation, in a decisive 'no comment'. *The Sunday Times* carried on checking. Vanunu's precious two-week deadline was almost up and there seemed no chance of an escape from the growing dangers of London.

On 23rd September, Vanunu wrote a crucial letter to John McKnight in Sydney. Still reluctant to let Vanunu out alone, *The Sunday Times* had used its own internal mail system to carry the letter to Australia. It was posted at Sydney's Kingsford Smith Airport and reached McKnight almost a week later. It read:

> Dear John,
>   I am sorry for not writing any letters. Now that I have finished work with the journalists and helped them to write the story, I have time to write and think about the future. The story is going to be published next Sunday 31.9 (*sic*). Now I think I am going to stay here for a few weeks to see what the reaction is and also to see if the Israelis are going to do somthing to me. I will try to do an application for citizenship here in Australia and other countries and I will see what the answer is.

Vanunu signed himself 'John Crossman', the baptismal name he had adopted at St John's.

The letter clearly shows that Vanunu expected that *The Sunday Times* would publish his story a week before they actually did. It leaves no doubt that Vanunu knew the Israelis would soon be onto him. But Vanunu had made up his mind to stay where he was, despite the risks. That decision was the one thing that might have saved him from the Mossad.

CHAPTER SEVEN

VANUNU MET CINDY ON WEDNESDAY 24TH
SEPTEMBER. Cindy said she was an American
beautician. The meeting took place in Leicester
Square, in London's West End, and demonstrated the
clinical efficiency that was to characterise the Mossad
kidnapping operation from the beginning. Subtly catch-
ing his attention without appearing to do so, Cindy
coaxed the usually shy Vanunu to approach her. They
began chatting and carried on their conversation over
coffee. Vanunu had been left to make all the running
himself. Demoralised and anxious for company, Vanunu
fell for the lure of a woman who seemed as shy as he
was.

It was scarcely a fortnight since Vanunu had fled from
the bar of the Sydney Hilton after being approached by
two men he didn't know. With his story nearing publication, he was now more vulnerable than ever. Why, at
such a critical moment, did he allow himself to be
befriended by a complete stranger?

Part of the answer lies with the stranger herself.
Cindy was far from being the reticent blonde Vanunu
took her for. She was in fact a Mossad agent. Her real
identity remained a mystery until finally, a year later,

The Sunday Times tracked her down to the Israeli town of Netanya, where she lived with her husband Ofer Bentov, a major in Israeli military intelligence. Cindy's real name was Cheryl. She had taken the name 'Cindy Hanin' from her sister-in-law.

Cheryl Bentov had been born and brought up in the United States, where she became actively involved in Jewish politics. Her parents had a messy divorce, and Cheryl looked to her rabbi, Dov Kentof, for support. It was his encouragement that sent Cheryl to Israel for a three-month course, partly funded by the World Zionist Organisation, on Jewish history. When Cheryl finished high school she returned to Israel, where she was recruited by Nahal, an elite military youth organisation established to help build and defend new settlements.

With the seventeen years she had spent in the United States, Cheryl Bentov was the ideal agent for the Mossad operation. An approach by an Israeli woman in London would have made even Vanunu suspicious. The Mossad sent her to London, where she booked into the Eccleston Hotel in Victoria.

Vanunu kept his friendship with Cindy secret from the people at *The Sunday Times*. By the time they found out about it, Vanunu had been won over. For a week the pair met daily. Vanunu gave up even the most basic security precautions and gave Cindy the telephone number of his hotel and the name under which he was registered. Cindy left numerous calls for him. Although falling deeper and deeper under Cindy's influence, Vanunu never mentioned her. But a *Sunday Times* reporter, Max Prangnell, waiting in a taxi to take Vanunu to the office, caught sight of Cindy outside the Tate Gallery. He described her as in her mid twenties, about 5 ft 8 ins, plump, with bleached blonde hair, thick lips, a brown trilby style hat, brown tweed trouser suit, high heels and probably Jewish. *The Sunday Times* used this description to portray Cindy as a blonde mata hari who lured Vanunu to Rome with the promise of sex.

Vanunu was feeling intensely lonely when he met Cindy. Robin Morgan, then features editor at *The Sunday Times*, observed in him a desperate need for female company and believed he would have followed Cindy to Rome for that reason. Others, such as Peter Hounam, were less sure. At the age of thirty-two, Vanunu had little or no sexual experience. While in Australia he spoke of having a girlfriend, Judy Zimmet, an American nurse he met in Israel who had since returned to Boston. But their relationship was not a strong one. On Vanunu's side it seemed more idealised than real. Vanunu had spoken to David Smith in vague terms about wanting to settle down one day with a 'nice girl', but he did not specify anybody. William Kinbacher, who shared a flat with Vanunu in Sydney, said that he went out occasionally with girls, but only in groups. David Smith is certain that Vanunu was not involved in a sexual relationship during the time he was in Sydney.

It is not hard to see Vanunu, the product of a rigidly conservative Jewish orthodox upbringing, inexperienced with women and abruptly separated from the people who had helped him find a new spiritual meaning to his life, falling suddenly and recklessly under the influence of a woman who seemed to offer him the friendship he craved. Mata hari or not, Cindy knew exactly how to behave towards Vanunu so as to win his trust and prise him away from the weakening grip of *The Sunday Times*. There is, however, no evidence that he ever had sex with Cindy.

Even without Cindy, Vanunu's reluctance to remain in hiding was making it increasingly difficult to look after him. Every day he spent in England put him at greater risk, but it was virtually impossible to protect him without a round-the-clock guard, which Vanunu refused to consider.

As the days passed, Cindy played on the reluctance of *The Sunday Times* to go ahead and publish. She claimed to have journalistic contacts of her own in Italy, and tried to convince Vanunu he would stand a better chance in Europe. Vanunu was wavering, but hadn't made up his mind to leave.

On Sunday 28th September, five days after engineering her meeting with Vanunu, Cindy had an extraordinary piece of luck. Vanunu's supposed partner, Oscar Guerrero, fearing he would never see the $US 25,000 promised by *The Sunday Times*, had walked out on him and delivered his version of the story and several photographs of Dimona to the rival *Sunday Mirror*. Most damaging of all, he had given the paper an up-to-date picture of Vanunu. Cindy drew Mordechai's attention to the article, and Vanunu was horrified to find his photograph splashed across the inside pages of a newspaper selling millions of copies throughout Britain.

Guerrero's motive was not just money. Tony Frost, the news editor of *The Sunday Mirror*, said that Guerrero originally asked for £200,000 for his story.[25] *The Sunday Mirror*, scenting a cleverly disguised rat behind Guerrero's photographs of himself in the company of President Alfonsin, Prime Minister Peres and the rest, refused. Guerrero's price plummetted to £25,000. His prime motive, said Frost, was revenge. He wanted to get back at *The Sunday Times* for turning Vanunu against him.

The story was a windfall for *The Sunday Mirror*, and it made good use of it to pour scorn on *The Sunday Times*. The headline was 'THE STRANGE CASE OF ISRAEL AND THE NUCLEAR CONMAN'.

A typed letter purporting to be from *The Sunday*

Times referred to 'an agreement with Mr Guerrero' preventing the paper from publishing details 'obtained through his efforts from an interview with an Israeli scientist'. The description of Vanunu as a scientist was taken from Oscar Guerrero's initial approach to *The Sunday Times*, before Vanunu had the chance to correct Guerrero's numerous distortions. The extract was printed under a prominent picture of *The Sunday Times* masthead.

The Sunday Mirror, without the time for the arduous scientific checks carried out by *The Sunday Times*, and convinced that Guerrero himself was a fraud, wasted no time in following up its hunch, and produced a story that seemingly demolished Vanunu's credibility by exposing Guerrero as a charlatan with a police record and a string of journalistic hoaxes to his name.

The Sunday Mirror didn't mention Israel's 200-warhead nuclear arsenal, but led instead with the claim that Israel had successfully manufactured five neutron bombs. The claim was attributed not to Vanunu, but to Guerrero himself, described by *The Sunday Mirror*, with its tongue firmly in its cheek, as a '36-year-old globe-trotting South American journalist'.

'The bomb is the world's deadliest weapon,' declared *The Sunday Mirror*, raking up the controversy that had long surrounded US development of the weapon. 'It can wipe out humans with a massive dose of radiation, while leaving buildings intact.'

The Sunday Mirror, obviously, was far more interested in exposing Guerrero as a fraud than it was in analysing Israel's nuclear armoury. Announcing that 'grave doubts' existed about the authenticity of the story—hardly surprising in view of Guerrero's flimsy grasp of the evidence—the paper asked:

'Could Guerrero's story be a hoax, or even something

more sinister—a plot to discredit Israel, with him acting as an agent in dis-information?'

From that point, *The Sunday Mirror* proceeded to lampoon both Guerrero and Vanunu, repeating Guerrero's boast that he had uncovered 'the biggest story since Watergate', describing the way he had 'reeled off a Who's Who of eminent journalists who were "good friends" of his', and printing with unmistakable relish his claim to have been 'double crossed ... by men from *The Sunday Times* newspaper'.

Vanunu fared even worse. Ludicrously identified by Guerrero as 'Israeli nuclear physicist Professor Mordechai Vanunu', his decision to reveal the secrets of Dimona was explained as an attempt 'to force Israel to the negotiating table with the Arabs and the PLO'.

If it had wanted more material with which to undermine Guerrero's story, *The Sunday Mirror* found it in his account of his meeting with Vanunu in Sydney. Glossing over his time as a fence painter, Guerrero had concocted a more distinguished occupation for himself. *The Sunday Mirror* found it 'bizarre'.

'I was in Australia writing a book,' said Guerrero. 'Vanunu approached me out of the blue. Friends in Israel had given him my name and address ... he told me he was a scientist who had played an important part in Israel's nuclear programme.'

Tossing a final dart at its Sunday rival, *The Sunday Mirror* reported Guerrero's claims that he had been 'cut out' of the deal by *The Sunday Times*.

'I was angry and phoned *The Sunday Times*,' Guerrero was quoted as saying. 'They told me to "get lost". They treated me like dirt.'

Printing several of Oscar Guerrero's celebrity photographs across the top of the story, *The Sunday Mirror* said that photographic experts were sceptical about their authenticity, and had identified faults in the 'focusing, scale and alignment' of the photographs. (*The Sunday Times*, using its own tests, had discovered that at least one of the photographs was authentic and was an agency picture taken in Canberra. Some, although not proved to be fakes, suggested that Guerrero had simply managed to elbow himself into the pictures. Others were clearly fakes, made by superimposing pictures of Guerrero onto photographs of international leaders meeting the press.)

The Sunday Mirror also reproduced pictures of Dimona and certain components of what it called the 'Doomsday device'. By then the story had been so thoroughly discredited that it was almost superfluous to invite independent experts to complete the job, but *The Sunday Mirror* did it anyway. It quoted Dr John Baruch, described as a research fellow at Leeds University, who concluded that the photographs were 'a reasonably well-informed hoax', that could have been taken inside any laboratory anywhere in the world, and might just as easily have come from a car wash or an egg factory. A second, unnamed 'expert' told the newspaper that the configuration of components shown in the photographs would probably blow the place apart. Both experts were reported to have made much of one photograph of a sealed cabinet full of gloves. They pointed to the use of poisonous, but not radioactive materials, said the two experts.

Recalling the story, Baruch now says: 'When *The Sunday Mirror* contacted me I acted on the assumption that *The Sunday Mirror* and the journalists concerned were disinterested parties. The evidence they gave me was that a set of photographs that they had acquired were allegedly of a nuclear bomb-making plant taken by a technician at the plant.'

The photographs handed to Baruch comprised only a fraction of those later given to Dr Frank Barnaby. They were, as well, only black-and-white reproductions of the original colour photographs. Baruch said that the pictures shown to him fell into four groups: exteriors of a building that could have been a nuclear reactor, views across a desert, disassembled spherical parts that credibly could have formed the components of a small nuclear bomb and lastly a facility for machining toxic materials. Baruch remembers all the photographs being blurred.

The Sunday Mirror journalist went to Baruch's home with the photographs and quickly spread them before him. In less than two hours he had gone, taking his story with him.

Baruch says that there was no evidence that the materials in the photographs were plutonium, uranium or berylium apart from a 'rather blurred radioactive hazard sign'. He told the journalist that it 'might be a nuclear manufacturing facility'. He maintains that the evidence he was shown was 'insufficient to state with certainty that the photographs were taken at a nuclear bomb-making facility'. Disturbed by a number of aspects of the photographs, Baruch was convinced that if the story was a hoax, it was a highly sophisticated one.

The resulting article in *The Sunday Mirror* glossed over Baruch's cautious assessment of the photographs he had seen. Baruch stoically accepts this as 'regrettable journalistic licence'. As soon as he saw Vanunu's revelations in *The Sunday Times*, Baruch says he was 'convinced there was a nuclear bomb factory in the Negev'. He nevertheless defends his own assessment as the only one he could have made, given the evidence he was shown.

'I regard Frank Barnaby as a competent physicist and I trust him,' he says. On the question of the truth of Vanunu's allegations, Baruch says: 'There are lots of questions which a competent physicist would ask

Vanunu. I assume Barnaby asked these questions and was convinced by the answers.'

The Sunday Mirror, however, had demolished the claims put forward by Oscar Guerrero, and Vanunu, by association, had seen his own credibility ruined. After such a damaging assault on an already risky story, *The Sunday Times* could hardly have been expected to go ahead and publish. It was just the opportunity that the Mossad had been waiting for, and they wasted no time in seizing it.

Within hours of discovering his story in *The Sunday Mirror,* Vanunu had told *The Sunday Times* that he wanted to drop the existing security arrangements and disappear into the crowd. Cindy had little difficulty convincing him of the dangers of staying in London with his picture all over the newspapers, but had not yet persuaded him to leave the country.

The Israeli Embassy had confirmed one important fact. While denying the existence of a Professor Vanunu, it did acknowledge that a junior technician called Vanunu had worked for the Israeli Atomic Energy Commission. *The Sunday Times* could finally be sure of Vanunu's identity, but it was still holding back from publishing the story. As deadlines came and went, Vanunu worried that even now, with his identity exposed, the paper might decide to abandon the project.

At about 1 am GMT on the morning of Tuesday 30th September, 1986, Vanunu made a desperate call to John McKnight at St John's Rectory in Kings Cross. McKnight's secretary took the call, and told Vanunu that McKnight was out, probably at the house of another clergyman, Stephen Gray. Vanunu sounded desperate to speak to McKnight. He took down Gray's telephone number. He called Gray, but McKnight was not there. Vanunu told Gray he had been to the headquarters of *The Sunday Times* at Wapping. He said he had argued with the paper over its delay in publishing his story. Vanunu was also furious with Guerrero for passing his photograph to *The Sunday Mirror*. He was isolated, and felt that he could no longer trust *The Sunday Times* to look after his interests. Gray sensed that Vanunu had reached a crisis. Recalling Vanunu's mood during that last call, Gray describes him as 'alone, worried, disturbed and disillusioned'. He was 'caught between what he felt he must do according to his conscience and what that meant for his relationship with his country and his family. He was a torn person'.

Distressed at not being able to reach McKnight, Vanunu put down the phone. At 9 am he put through a call to Peter Hounam at *The Sunday Times*. Hounam, the Insight reporter whom Vanunu trusted most, was aware of Vanunu's fears. The Insight team was itself frustrated at what had begun to seem like stonewalling on the part of executives on the paper. Their over-cautiousness was understandable. By publishing Vanunu's story, *The Sunday Times* was putting at stake the credibility it had struggled to regain after the Hitler Diaries fiasco. *Stern*, the German magazine which had bought the faked diaries in the first place, had seen its circulation drop by more than a million as a result of publishing them. *The Sunday Times* was not prepared to risk another catastrophic loss of face.

In exposing Guerrero, *The Sunday Mirror* had undermined the whole Dimona story. *The Sunday Mirror* had run only scraps of the real story—the scraps Guerrero had chosen to tell—and much of what it printed was false. Everything about the story now looked tainted. Senior figures on *The Sunday Times* had become openly sceptical about its background and unconvinced by the evidence gathered in support of it. The contract had not even been signed.

As he listened to the stumbling phone call, Peter

Hounam sensed Vanunu's fear. Hounam had already warned Vanunu that Cindy might be a Mossad plant, but Vanunu refused to believe him. Hounam had at last persuaded Vanunu to bring her to dinner with Hounam and his wife on Tuesday evening. Vanunu was now reneging on the agreement. He told Hounam he was going 'into the country', or perhaps 'out of the country', for a couple of days while things cooled down. Vanunu's English was poor, and Hounam couldn't make out the exact words. In any case, Hounam was dismayed at the thought of Vanunu leaving London. He tried to talk him out of it. When that failed, he pressed Vanunu to tell him where he was going. Vanunu wouldn't say.

Hounam reminded him he was yet to sign his contract. Without that, *The Sunday Times* would be left in the invidious position of having either to abandon the story, or to run it without Vanunu's written permission. Even if it decided to publish without a signed contract, Vanunu's presence was essential for the carefully staged back-up interviews and press conferences the paper needed to support such a controversial story. Vanunu promised he would be back on Thursday to sign the contract. Realising that his efforts to dissuade Vanunu from leaving were getting nowhere, Hounam tried to stop him using anything that would give away his identity. He warned Vanunu not to show his passport, which would have been easily traceable through Interpol records, and not to use any of his credit cards. Most importantly, he told Vanunu not to leave Britain, where a series of recent events— notably the Hindawi trial, where Britain had sought EC sanctions against Syria for its alleged involvement in a plot to bring down a civilian airliner, and the Dikko affair, in which Israeli agents had been implicated in an attempt to smuggle a Nigerian diplomat out of Britain in a wooden crate—would make the Mossad wary about committing any act that might harm Anglo/Israeli relations.

Vanunu stressed that he would only be gone for a couple of days and promised to be back on Thursday to resolve the business about the contract. Then he hung up.

Whether Vanunu meant to tell Peter Hounam that he was going 'out of the country' or 'into the country', he was now on the verge of making up his mind, or had made up his mind already, to disregard Hounam's advice and leave Britain. Knowing all that he knew about the danger he faced, and with Hounam's warning fresh in his mind, it is scarcely possible that Vanunu could have reached that decision alone. By leaving the relative sanctuary of Britain, Vanunu would be delivering himself into the hands of the Mossad agents assigned to capture him. But by the time he made his last call to Peter Hounam, Mordechai Vanunu was no longer in control of his own fate.

From the moment Vanunu made his decision to hide in the London crowds, Cindy started talking him out of it. On Monday 29th September, Cindy forced Vanunu's hand by buying an air ticket to Rome. It was a business class ticket, bought for £426 from Thomas Cook in Berkeley Street, not far from Leicester Square. She was going, she said, to her sister's apartment in Rome. She offered Vanunu a last chance to join her. Sometime between then and Tuesday morning, Vanunu agreed. At 10.30 am, only an hour after he had finished speaking to Hounam, Vanunu checked out of the Mountbatten Hotel and went with Cindy to Heathrow Airport. Cindy paid for his ticket. Disguising himself as a European citizen, Vanunu was not required to show any proof of his identity and passed through the gate without leaving a trace. At 2.10 pm the pair boarded British Airways flight BA504, landing at Leonardo da Vinci Airport, just outside Rome, at 6.28 pm. Photocopies of the tickets showed Vanunu had used his own name.

CHAPTER EIGHT

THE THURSDAY DEADLINE PASSED for signing the contract, and there was no trace of Vanunu. He had failed to contact anyone either in London or Sydney. Roger Wilsher of *The Sunday Times* rang John McKnight in Sydney to find out if he had heard anything.

The Sunday Times had seen a copy of the telephone calls Vanunu had made from the hotel, and they knew that Vanunu had been ringing McKnight regularly. They also knew about the letters McKnight had given Vanunu before he left Australia. One was to the rector of St Helen's Bishopsgate, the Revd Dick Lucas, a friend of McKnight's, saying that Vanunu was a trustworthy parishioner and asking him if he would give him help if he needed it. The other was an open letter to any Anglican clergyman, which said essentially the same thing.

Wilsher sounded anxious and asked McKnight to get in touch with his friend at St Helen's Bishopsgate to see if Vanunu had contacted him for help. When McKnight asked him what was wrong, Wilsher said that there had been tension with Vanunu on the Monday before he disappeared, and that Vanunu had said that he needed to go away to think about things. He mentioned the story in *The Sunday Mirror* and told McKnight that Vanunu had seemed very nervous. He said Vanunu feared that his credibility had been ruined by the half-cocked story Guerrero had given to *The Sunday Mirror*.

McKnight rang St Helen's Bishopsgate and All Souls' Langham Place. No one had heard of Mordechai Vanunu. Then he rang the parish of St Martin-in-the-Fields, where Vanunu had been to a recital. They knew nothing about Vanunu. McKnight rang Roger Wilsher and told him. Wilsher was disappointed, but said that McKnight should contact him immediately if Vanunu called. He said *The Sunday Times* was reluctant to publish without Vanunu's express permission. As the Sunday deadline approached, *The Sunday Times* rang three more times, but McKnight was unable to tell them anything.

McKnight's concern was not for the story but for Vanunu. If he was in danger, McKnight wanted the police to know about it. *The Sunday Times* was reluctant to report Vanunu's disappearance. At that time no one knew if Vanunu had been kidnapped or had simply gone to ground. To alert the authorities and Mossad to the fact that Vanunu was missing might have given them an open invitation to pick him up. *The Sunday Times* was not prepared at this point to trust anybody with Vanunu's life.

When the Dimona story finally appeared on October 5th, *The Sunday Times* gave no hint that Vanunu might be in danger. For all anyone knew, he had simply vanished.

The person who finally persuaded *The Sunday Times* to publish was, ironically, the Israeli Prime Minister, Shimon Peres. Learning of the newspaper's intention to print Vanunu's account of Dimona, Peres convened the confidential Editors' Committee, a panel consisting of the editors of Israel's major newspapers. Peres announced that *The Sunday Times* was in possession of the Dimona story, and ordered the editors not to pass any comment on it in their own pages. A reporter on one of the papers, probably the Hebrew daily *Ha'aretz*, was instructed by his editor to confirm the story from London. He put through a call to *The Sunday Times*, in which he mentioned the Editors' Committee meeting ordered by Prime Minister Peres. It was this call that tipped off *The Sunday Times* that Vanunu's disclosures were genuine, and cleared the way for immediate publication. As Peter Hounam described it later: 'Whenever a journalist [in Israel] is getting close to an accurate story, someone from the censorship calls him to confirm by telling the reporter to stay away from the story.'

The Sunday Times published Mordechai Vanunu's story on its front page on 5th October 1986, without a signed contract. The headline was 'Revealed: the secrets of Israel's nuclear arsenal'. Inside, another headline ran right across pages four and five: 'Inside Dimona, Israel's nuclear bomb factory'. The strap line above it said: 'For many years its existence was suspected: now a technician who worked there tells the story of how his country has become a major nuclear power.'

Beside an elaborate three-dimensional diagram of the building called Machon 2, the report gave a stage-by-stage description of the plutonium extraction processes carried out at Dimona:

> Unit 10, a ground floor, drive-in delivery bay, received the trucks carrying the 100 large and 40 smaller fuel rods from the reactor core. A crane lowers the rods in baskets down through Level One which is a service floor, through Level Two which mainly houses the control room for the plant, to Unit 11 on Level Three. Here the uranium fuel rods containing the plutonium by-product are chemically stripped of their aluminium coating.

The story went on to explain, with precise details of weights and temperatures, how the uranium was then stripped and immersed in nitric acid, which was then heated to dissolve the uranium. The liquid was then treated to remove radioactivity, and mixed with a solution which separated out the plutonium from the uranium.

The Sunday Times described how the liquid was further concentrated, heated, cooled and mixed with hydrogen pyroxide and other chemicals to leave a plutonium 'cake', which was then baked in Unit 37.

The baking process concentrates the metal into a solid button weighing 130 grams. Nine buttons of plutonium were produced each week, 1.17 kilograms a week for the 34 weeks a year that the process ran. (It shut down for four months for repairs and maintenance.) The annual net result of this separation process is around 40 kilograms of plutonium a year, or nearly six times the most optimistic assessments of Israel's plutonium-making capabilities.

The Sunday Times also revealed that tritium was manufactured at Dimona, giving Israel the capacity to build thermonuclear weapons many times more powerful than conventional atomic bombs. Raw materials extracted at Dimona were machined into bomb parts which were then taken in a guarded convoy of trucks and cars to a secret location in Haifa. The report concluded that 'Israel ... produced enough plutonium for 100 nuclear bombs of at least 200 kilotons, equivalent to the one dropped on Nagasaki. By using sophisticated designs requiring smaller amounts of plutonium, it could have produced enough to make 200 nuclear bombs.'

This, said *The Sunday Times*, was enough to rank Israel as the world's sixth most powerful nuclear power, after the United States, the Soviet Union, Britain, France and China, and far ahead of those other countries, such as India, Pakistan and South Africa, suspected of having the bomb. Vanunu's testimony also indicated that Israel had the resources to build the neutron bomb.

An accompanying story drew on the testimony of several nuclear experts, both named and unnamed, to corroborate the story. Dr Frank Barnaby, a nuclear physicist who had worked at Britain's Aldermaston nuclear research site before becoming director of the Swedish Institute for peace research, cross-checked the results of his study of the evidence with three other experts in the field of nuclear science. Barnaby, said *The Sunday Times*, concluded that Vanunu's story was 'totally convincing'.

An exhaustive debriefing carried out by a team including Dr Barnaby had been submitted to scientists working in the British atomic energy industry. Summing up their verdict, one of the scientists said that after seeing the report and Vanunu's photographs he was 'more convinced than ever' that the claims were true.

Vanunu's testimony was also presented to Dr Theodore Taylor, an acknowledged world expert on nuclear weapons. Dr Taylor, a former head of the Pentagon's atomic weapons test programme and a student of the bomb's creator, Robert Oppenheimer, spent thirty-six hours studying pages of Vanunu's evidence and dozens of photographs. He told *The Sunday Times*:

> There should no longer be any doubt that Israel is, and for at least a decade has been, a fully fledged nuclear weapons state. The information obtained from Vanunu's statements and photographs as presented to me are entirely consistent with a present Israeli capacity to produce at least five to ten weapons a year that are significantly smaller, lighter and more efficient than the first types of nuclear weapons developed by the US, USSR, UK, France and China.

After close examination of photographs depicting a piece of lithium deuteride being machined into a hemispherical shell, as well as full-scale models of other components, Taylor and Barnaby independently reached the conclusion that the bomb being manufactured was not an ordinary atom bomb but a thermonuclear weapon capable of generating vast destructive power from relatively small amounts of plutonium. Some of the experts consulted by *The Sunday Times* were more sceptical, believing that the original reactor could not have been simply enlarged to produce the necessary amount of plutonium, but would have had to be completely rebuilt. They were also incredulous that Vanunu could have been left alone to take photographs in such a sensitive area, and were surprised that a mere technician should know so much about what was going on inside Dimona.

Summing up, *The Sunday Times* declared that the verdict of ten 'senior and expert scientists' was that 'Vanunu's testimony cannot be faulted'.

Reaction to the story was immediate, and the following day Vanunu's revelations appeared in scores of international newspapers. The news was reported widely on Israeli radio and television on the day it was published in London, and made the front page of *The Jerusalem Post* the next day. It was also reported in the seven Hebrew-language dailies, which until then had published nothing on Israel's nuclear arsenal. Strict censorship laws prevented the Israeli press from following up the story.

While Vanunu's revelations found space in newspapers, radio and television broadcasts around the world, it got hardly a mention in the British press. The reason, crowed *The Sunday Times*, was the reluctance of other Fleet Street editors to give it credit for a 'major international scoop'.

The initial coverage of the story in *The Jerusalem Post* was surprisingly frank, conveying a certain pride in the disclosure. 'Israel now sixth most powerful nuclear power,' the paper proclaimed between quotation marks the day after the story appeared in London, along with a second story: 'Behind the doors of "Machon 2"'. Scrupulously refraining from any comment on the allegations, *The Jerusalem Post* carried a single paragraph stating: Israeli officials refused last night to comment on *The Sunday Times* article, beyond referring to the Israel Atomic Energy Commission's established position that it declines to comment on publications about Israel's alleged military atomic capacity.

But for all the drama of Vanunu's revelations, and the damage they threatened to do to the fragile peace in the Middle East, they failed to hold the headlines. In Israel itself, jokes about the 'banana-bending factory' at Dimona reflected the popular belief that the country both possessed and needed to possess, and, above all, had a right to possess nuclear weapons. Dr Baruch Knei-Paz, an experienced observer of Israeli politics contacted by *The Sunday Times* after it published Vanunu's story, confirmed this when he told the paper: 'Most people here have assumed for some time that Israel had such bombs. . . . Let the Arabs know, and even better that it is not us who tells [them] but it comes in a roundabout way. Like through a report in *The Sunday Times*.'

The Israeli Government, satisfied by having its military might emphasised to belligerent Arab leaders, weathered the diplomatice storm behind its stock formula that it would not be the first to introduce nuclear weapons into the region.

Far from being damaged by Vanunu's revelations, Israel was clearly strengthened by the disclosure of its sophisticated technology. Had that been the end of the affair, Mordechai Vanunu himself might have been forgotten by the rest of the world. But in taking his country's military secrets to the foreign press, over which the government censors naturally had no control, Vanunu had set a precedent. It was a precedent that Shimon Peres was determined to stamp out.

By now McKnight knew that something had gone wrong. He contacted the Archbishop of Canterbury's office, who got in touch with Terry Waite, who was in France at the time. On his advice McKnight called the British Foreign Office. He spoke to the Assistant Under-secretary, the head of the Middle East desk, and the head of the Near East and North Africa desk. Each of them in turn put him onto someone else in the department. Finally they decided it was not a Foreign Office matter at all, and told McKnight to take it up with the Home Office. They gave him some names, but when he got onto the Home Office he was told that it was a matter for the police. The police told him it was a matter for the Foreign Office. Finally, after many hours of overseas telephone calls, McKnight decided he was getting nowhere from Australia, and hung up.

McKnight's main concern was to try to get Vanunu reported missing so that the police could start their investigations. For two days after Vanunu's story appeared, *The Sunday Times* held back from officially reporting him missing. With no evidence to the contrary, they presumed that Vanunu had merely gone to ground until the publicity surrounding his revelations had died down.

McKnight finally contacted the police himself. He was told that it was not possible for him to report Vanunu missing unless he was either in Britain or was a relative. McKnight had no way of reaching Vanunu's family and there was nobody he knew in England who was prepared to report him missing. He only had one other option, and that was to fly to London himself. If Vanunu had been alone or hiding somewhere, McKnight knew he would be wary of the media. He thought that it was just possible that Vanunu might try to contact him instead.

Before McKnight left Sydney, he decided to force the

issue by holding a press conference, at which he reported that Vanunu was missing and that he was on his way to London to try to make contact with him. He left Australia on Tuesday 7th October.

By the time McKnight touched down at Heathrow Airport, *The Sunday Times* had notified the local police at Holborn police station of Vanunu's disappearance. McKnight went straight to the Anglican Consultative Council, where he was contacted by three detectives from Scotland Yard's Special Branch, working at Holborn police station, who questioned him over Vanunu's disappearance. McKnight spoke for some time with the detectives, but could offer little hard information. It was now nine days since anyone had heard from Vanunu, and the police felt the trail was already cold. McKnight then went to the Wapping headquarters of *The Sunday Times*, where he met the Insight reporters Rowena Webster and Roger Wilsher, and the features editor, Robin Morgan.

McKnight found Robin Morgan less than enthusiastic to reveal any details about Vanunu's time in London or his disappearance. *The Sunday Times* still could not be sure whether Vanunu had gone to ground or had been kidnapped, and because of the delicacy of the situation were reluctant to share information.

The Anglican Diocesan officials were no more helpful than the Foreign Office. McKnight then went to St Martin-in-the-Fields. Staff there also refused to help for fear of reprisals, although they were evidently in some doubt as to who might carry out those reprisals. They told McKnight they were worried that Arab or Israeli terrorists might blow the place up. They didn't seem to know which. There was support from the vicar of St Mary's Kensington, the Revd Ian Robson, and the vicar of St Bride's, Fleet Street, Canon John Oates, and his staff.

McKnight was anxious to let Vanunu know he was in town, but was loath to publish a direct contact number that would lead the Mossad straight to him. He also wanted to avoid the risk of being inundated by cranks and others claiming to have seen Vanunu, so he devised a system whereby Vanunu could ring St John's in Sydney, and by giving his baptismal name—John Crossman—he would be told how to contact McKnight in London. Since his connection with Vanunu had already been widely reported, McKnight was asked by the hotel to register under the name of Mr Incognito, so as to avoid upsetting the hotel's wealthy Jewish and American patrons.

On 12th October, *The Sunday Times* published its follow-up story, recounting the sketchy facts of Vanunu's disappearance and including a lengthy interview with Professor Francis Perrin, the former head of France's nuclear programme, who confirmed many of the crucial details in Vanunu's original story. During the days following the second article, there was no word from Vanunu. McKnight knew Vanunu would have called if he'd had the chance. He was convinced Vanunu was in serious trouble.

The police had checked all exit slips at the airport and seaports, and found no sign of Vanunu having left the country. They then had to consider the possibility that Vanunu had been involved in an accident or that he had already been killed by the Mossad, and could therefore be lying injured in hospital without any identification. The police checked on nearby hospitals and morgues but found no trace of him. McKnight drew up a detailed description, which was circulated to morgues and hospitals all over the South of England. He heard nothing back.

The little evidence known to *The Sunday Times* at this time suggested that Vanunu was still in Britain. If he had already left, it must have been in a great hurry. Neither Vanunu nor anyone else had touched the account containing $US 40,000 in an American bank, which Vanunu held jointly with his brother, Meir. For some time before he left, Vanunu had been borrowing small amounts of money from people at *The Sunday Times*. He had little more than £100 on him when he left, just enough to pay for a few days' accommodation. Until then *The Sunday Times* had been paying his hotel bills. The paper believed that the cash Vanunu was carrying was not enough for him to travel abroad, and he would have needed to draw on his US bank account. A week after his disappearance, when his account had still not been touched, the evidence seemed overwhelming that Vanunu had been abducted and was being held against his will, or had been murdered.

Other Fleet Street newspapers showed little interest in Vanunu's disappearance until the American magazine *Newsweek* suddenly hurled the story back onto the front pages. The *Newsweek* report, dated 20th October and cabled around the world by all the major news services, said that Vanunu had been captured by Israeli agents and was now awaiting a secret trial in Israel. Sources said to be 'close to the Israeli intelligence community' told *Newsweek*'s Jerusalem correspondent, Milan Kubic, that the Mossad had carried out a sophisticated land-and-sea operation to get Vanunu. They claimed that a woman was used to lure Vanunu onto a yacht in the Mediterranean and that once in international waters the yacht was intercepted by Mossad agents and taken back aboard a high-speed boat to Israel.

The report was eagerly grabbed by newspapers which had ignored the Dimona story. On the day the *Newsweek* account appeared, the London *Evening Standard* paper published the story across its front page under the headline: 'A-BOMB "SPY" IN KIDNAP.'

'Israelis snatch man who offered secrets in London,' proclaimed the *Standard*, describing the operation as 'an audacious snatch reminiscent of the kidnap of war criminal Adolf Eichmann'.

While standing by its claim that Vanunu was being held in Israel, *Newsweek* was less than certain of the dramatic account it had given of his abduction. Journalists in Tel Aviv and Jerusalem were reported as having known of his capture some days before, but of having been prevented by the Israeli censor from reporting it. Israeli intelligence sources dismissed the *Newsweek* story as 'rubbish'.

McKnight decided to leave England immediately for Israel. Phoning the Israeli Embassy in London, McKnight expressed his concern for Vanunu and asked if, as Vanunu's priest, he would be able to visit him if he was being held in prison. The embassy staff assured him that Vanunu, like any other Israeli citizen, had certain rights, and that if he should want a minister of his choice to visit him, that would be allowed. They said nothing concrete to indicate they knew where Vanunu was, but McKnight believed he had been given an implicit acknowledgement that Vanunu was at that moment in custody in Israel.

Arriving at St George's Cathedral in Jerusalem, McKnight was warned by Canon Naim Atik of the sensitivity of the relationship between the Anglican Church in Israel, the Palestinians and the Israelis. Atik promised that the church would offer McKnight any help that it could.

The signs of concern and encouragement McKnight found in his meeting with Canon Atik were not shown by other Anglicans in Israel. The Anglican Church, nervous about Jewish reprisals if it ventured into the political minefield surrounding Israel's defence policy, quickly backed away from its initial offers of help. The dean of St George's, who had been overseas during McKnight's meeting with Canon Atik, was less than thrilled to find the burly figure of McKnight stirring up trouble in his parish. McKnight was advised to distance himself from the Anglican Church, on the grounds that support given to someone who was actively sympathetic to Vanunu would bring discredit upon the Anglican Church in Israel. Vanunu's case would provoke similar divisions among the parishioners of McKnight's own church.

McKnight himself had been photographed and kept under surveillance from the moment he walked out of the airport. An Israeli government official, Arieh Meked, admitted as much when McKnight rang the Prime Minister's office seeking information about Vanunu.

Meked: How did you get on to me?
McKnight: I rang the operator.
Meked: But why did she put you through to me?
McKnight: Evidently you are the person who knows most about Mordechai Vanunu.
Meked: I know nothing about Mordechai Vanunu. I can't tell you anything about him.
McKnight: Then why was I put on to you?
Meked: Who are you? How did you get through to me?
McKnight: I'm John McKnight. I'm Mordechai's priest.
Meked: I know who you are. I have a picture of you lying on my desk right now.

Changing his story, Arieh Meked then asked McKnight to ring him back in a couple of days when he implied that he might have some information. McKnight tried

97

calling other government officials, but was always given the same answer—the Israeli Government knew nothing about the whereabouts of Mordechai Vanunu.

While he was in Jerusalem, McKnight was besieged by newspaper reporters from inside and outside Israel, particularly from Australia. When McKnight switched lodgings, a report was published in Australia saying that he had mysteriously disappeared from his Jerusalem hotel. McKnight sensed a great deal of anger inside Israel over what Vanunu had done, especially over his conversion to Christianity.

He organised a press conference in an attempt to increase pressure on the Israelis to release some information about what had happened to Vanunu. McKnight said he was sure that Vanunu was already back in Israel. The Israeli censor banned reporting of the meeting, but the press conference generated intense interest in the Israeli and foreign media. McKnight was approached by journalists who could put him in touch with officials dealing with the case, and who could tell him which prison Vanunu was being held in, which judge he had been before and who had been allowed to see him. Contact with the Israeli media was dangerous for both parties. Any Israeli journalist caught dealing with security secrets risked a heavy jail sentence. However, with no comment from inside the Israeli Government, the media offered McKnight his only source of information.

A journalist telephoned McKnight and asked if they could meet. The rendezvous took place in one of the seedy backstreets of Jerusalem quite close to the US Embassy. McKnight had left his clerical collar behind and arrived for the meeting in a collar and tie, wearing trenchcoat, glasses and hat. For half an hour he wandered up and down the street in the darkness. The only movement came from a car driving slowly by in the distance, and then turning round and coming back. Deciding that nobody was going to come, McKnight started walking towards the lights of the main street. Suddenly a car's headlights flashed, and a car pulled up beside him. McKnight recognised the driver as a journalist he had met a couple of days earlier. McKnight got into the car and they drove off quickly to shake off anyone who might have been watching. The man was thinly built, in his late twenties, and claimed to work for a Hebrew language newspaper. He spoke quietly, almost whispering. He claimed that he had spoken to someone who had seen Vanunu. He told McKnight that Vanunu was being held in a maximum security prison in Gedera, near Rehevot, and that his remand had been extended by a judge brought to his cell.

According to later reports in the British press, Vanunu's name had been accidentally included on a public list of those who had been remanded in custody the previous day. All other documents on the case were allegedly in the personal safe of Judge Aharon Simcha, who was believed to have been entrusted with the case.

London's *Financial Times* later quoted 'well-informed Israeli security sources' confirming that Vanunu was being held in Gedera.

McKnight proposed visiting Vanunu's family, but gave up the idea because of the intense media interest it was bound to generate. He did, however, phone the family from Jerusalem. Vanunu's father had been widely reported in the Israeli media as disowning his son and denouncing him as a traitor. McKnight, however, heard a quite different story. 'The family was supportive of Mordy,' McKnight says. 'They said he was still their son. They were shocked, but they knew he had a good reason for doing what he did. They told me they were grateful for my help.'

Still without a reply from the Israeli Government,

McKnight decided there was nothing more he could find out. He held another press conference. This time he was able to give a precise account of what was happening to Vanunu and where he was being held. After the second press conference, McKnight left the country. Although the media ban on McKnight's press statement remained, the information could not be suppressed once McKnight had carried it out of the country, and the Israeli censor soon lifted the ban.

Driving to Tel Aviv airport in one of the stretched eight-seater taxis commonly seen in Jerusalem, McKnight was joined in the car by seven other people, all orthodox Jews. 'They recognised me instantly,' said McKnight. 'None of them dared speak, not even the driver. We travelled in silence all the way to the airport.'

Arriving back in Australia, McKnight was met by Stephen Gray, who told him some extraordinary news about the man who had informed ASIO about Vanunu. Since telling ASIO of Vanunu's intention to reveal Israel's nuclear secrets, the ASIO informant had begun to regret his actions. Fearing that the information he had given ASIO might have reached the Mossad and led directly to Vanunu's kidnapping, or even his death, he had gone to St John's and told Gray what he had done. Gray, although in regular contact with McKnight while he was out of the country, had kept the information to himself until McKnight got back to Sydney. In the same Tarago minibus in which they had taken Vanunu to the airport six weeks before, Gray told McKnight that ASIO knew of Vanunu's plans. Half an hour later, at a packed press conference in the rectory lounge at St John's, McKnight announced that ASIO might have been involved in Vanunu's disappearance.

Within two days, ASIO had been in contact with McKnight. An ASIO officer came to the church to talk to him. He told McKnight that ASIO taped all its phone calls and kept a detailed record of all the information it received. He assured McKnight that ASIO had not passed on its information either to British intelligence or to the Mossad. ASIO got in touch with McKnight on two further occasions, both times to stress that it had not passed information about Vanunu to Britain's or anyone else's intelligence services. *The Sunday Times*, checking with intelligence sources in the UK, declared it '100 per cent certain' that ASIO routinely passed information to MI6 when it involved Britain.

On 13th November 1986, three questions were asked in the Australian Senate about ASIO's role in the Vanunu affair. The questioner, Senator Mason, asked whether ASIO had passed on any information it had received about Vanunu to 'the Israeli, British or any other security service', and whether there was any evidence suggesting that Mordechai Vanunu had broken Australian law during his visit. It took three months for the Attorney-General, Senator Evans, to produce a reply. On 17th February 1987, Evans said that as far as ASIO was concerned, 'it has been the established practice of successive Australian Governments to neither confirm nor deny the activities of that organisation'. Evans said he was not aware that Vanunu had broken any laws while in Australia.

Continuing allegations in British newspapers about ASIO's role in the Vanunu affair came to a head in August 1987, with a front page story in *The Sunday Times* entitled: 'How Israeli agents snatched Vanunu'. In the article, *The Sunday Times* stated decisively that 'the Australian Security Intelligence Organisation notified Britain's MI6 and when the plane landed at Heathrow on 12th September, two special branch officers were watching'. After hearing of the article, the Director-General of ASIO, Alan Wrigley, made an extraordinary public denial of ASIO's involvement. Wrigley said: 'It would appear that the London *Sunday Times* has fallen victim of its own or someone else's cheque book journalism. I deny absolutely that ASIO passed information to any foreign agency on Mr Vanunu's departure from Australia.'

A spokesman for ASIO said that although it was normal for the organisation to pass information to allied intelligence services, Wrigley's 'fairly categorical denial' meant that in Vanunu's case, it hadn't.

Alan Wrigley's 'fairly categorical denial' was, in fact, an unprecedented departure from ASIO's policy of refusing to comment on its operations. It had all the hallmarks of a man trying to browbeat the public into disbelieving a highly embarrassing, but entirely accurate, disclosure.

CHAPTER NINE

WITH MCKNIGHT OUT OF ISRAEL, rumours about Vanunu's fate continued to sweep the country. At one point, Vanunu was reported to be dead, the victim of a staged road accident. Other reports suggested that he was in hiding and would only reappear months later when the media had lost interest. He was reported to have been drugged and bundled out of Paris aboard an El Al jet. He was accused of being part of an Anglican plot against Israel. He was reputed to have fallen foul of international media magnate Rupert Murdoch, and to have been delivered to the Mossad to prevent rival news organisations from getting hold of his story. Another report—the first mention of a conspiracy theory that was to resurface in many guises as different people tried to explain away the mystery of his disappearance—was that Vanunu had actually been recruited by the Mossad to plant information about Israel's nuclear armoury, and was now celebrating his success. Rumours about Vanunu undergoing plastic surgery in a secret Mossad clinic left a plausible theory looking absurd.

In the months following his disappearance, as the details of Vanunu's story revealed the extraordinary lapse in Israeli security procedures, the belief grew that Vanunu had actually been an unwitting tool of a government-ordered conspiracy. The idea that the security forces could have just blundered—that a known left-wing sympathiser could have walked into Dimona with a camera and skipped out of the country with Israel's most valuable secrets in the bottom of a ruck-sack—seemed incredible. As the weeks dragged on, the key figures in the story—the only ones who knew the secret of Vanunu's abduction—said nothing. Freed from the blanket restriction imposed by the censor, the Israeli media began to challenge the Government over its refusal to speak, while at the same time defying the right of foreigners, and especially McKnight, to inter-fere in the matter.

In an editorial dated 28th October 1986, *The Jerusalem Post* wrote:

> Israel owes Rev McKnight no explanation and the premier is surely under no obligation to arrange a meeting for him with Vanunu, assuming the latter is in the country. But the question is whether Yitzhak Shamir may not owe it to the people of Israel to be more forthcoming in the matter of Vanunu.... The spokesman of the Prime Minister's Office was not believable and making a fool of the premier, when he protested on Sunday that 'we do not know anything about this matter'.... Telling obvious, and therefore, stupid, lies is neither a viable political option, nor a patrio-tic duty.

Other, equally indignant editorials appeared during the next fortnight. As reporters raked over Vanunu's record of subversive activity at university, the political backlash turned against the security services.

In the Knesset, the Anglican Church came under fire. One member, Avraham Verdiger, tried to place on the agenda an urgent motion alleging that Anglican missionary activity in Israel was at the root of the affair and calling for the confiscation of all Anglican property in Israel. The motion was rejected by the Knesset presidium. The right-wing member Geula Cohen planned to ask Prime Minister Yitzhak Shamir how Vanunu could have held onto a senior position at Dimona after his pro-Palestinian views became known by the authorities, and why disciplinary action wasn't taken against the people who failed to get rid of him. Cohen was allegedly pressured by the Prime Minister's office into dropping her question.

In his first public comment on Vanunu, in a radio interview on Radio Israel on 4th November, Shamir said: 'The Israeli Government will say what it finds fit to say, and it will fulfil its duty to its citizens.' He added that the 'Government has its own considerations' in avoiding public comment on the case.

If the Israeli Government was having a tough time hiding its knowledge of Vanunu's disappearance, the British Government of Margaret Thatcher was having a much tougher one proclaiming its ignorance. Finally, on Sunday 9th November, the Israeli Government admitted publicly that Vanunu was back in the country awaiting trial. The timing of the statement was clearly related to the political storm raging in Britain, and was intended to shore up Thatcher's denial over the weekend that she knew about Israel's intention of kidnapping Vanunu on British soil. On Saturday, *The Financial Times* had reported that former Prime Minister Shimon Peres had telephoned Thatcher and directly or indirectly informed her that Israel was about to kidnap Vanunu. Thatcher, according to the newspaper, gave her consent to the operation.

In a short statement, the Israeli Cabinet Secretary said that 'the Government of Israel announces that Mordechai Vanunu is legally under arrest in Israel, in accordance with a court order following a hearing in which a lawyer of his selection was present'.

The statement declared that 'all the rumours to the effect that Vanunu was "kidnapped" on English soil are without foundation'. While not denying that Peres had been in touch with the British Prime Minister over the affair, the statement said there was 'no basis for the report that Mr Peres contacted Mrs Thatcher in order to tell her about something that did not happen'. It did not deny *The Financial Times* report that Peres had informed Thatcher some days before publication that *The Sunday Times* was preparing to publish Vanunu's revelations.

Announcing that Vanunu's case was now *sub judice*, the statement made it clear that the Government had nothing more to say. Sources quoted in the Israeli press suggested that the statement was not put to the Cabinet, but was worked out by Prime Minister Shamir, Foreign Minister Peres and Defence Minister Rabin, without consulting other ministers. Although the release of the statement was largely backed by the Likud party in the Knesset, there was still concern about the damage that international speculation over Vanunu's kidnapping was doing to Israel's standing abroad, and particularly in Britain.

The day after the government announcement, Knesset member Ehud Olmert was quoted in *The Jerusalem Post* as saying: 'The Government had to respond to mounting international pressure, particularly from Britain, as to the exact circumstances of Vanunu's disappearance from Britain.' Like many others in Israel and overseas, Olmert took it for granted that the statement released by the Government was only a preface to a full explanation.

'Ultimately the Government will have to provide explanations as to the exact way in which Vanunu was taken into custody,' Olmert said.

Others, concerned about the security risk of providing more information, wanted the story to end with the statement. Likud Knesset faction chairman Sarah Doron spoke for many when she said: 'The Government did well by making public the fact that he is in Israeli custody, as the foreign press was full of the story anyhow. I hope that the entire affair will disappear from the media now. After all, we provide new sensations daily.'

The immediate repercussions of the statement threatened to do more damage to Israel than the exposure of its nuclear arsenal. Far from pacifying irate British MPs, it fuelled the diplomatic row with the Thatcher Government, at that time Israel's staunchest ally in Europe. At the Hindawi trial a month before, Syria had been caught red-handed sponsoring a terrorist plot to blow up an airliner in mid-air. Britain had broken off relations with Syria over the incident and had pressured its reluctant European Community partners into taking action against the PLO and Arab nations found guilty of supporting terrorism. Antagonising Britain, and particularly Mrs Thatcher, would have left the Israelis isolated in Europe.

With its web of ambiguous denials and silences, the statement gave the press greater incentive to speculate on the many rumours concerning how Vanunu was brought back to Israel. It explicitly denied that a kidnapping had taken place on British soil. Implicitly, it repudiated the rumour that Vanunu had been smuggled out of Britain as diplomatic baggage in an airlifted wooden crate. That left open a number of less flagrant and scarcely less illegal possibilities. Specifically, it failed to rebuff the *Newsweek* report that Vanunu had been enticed by Israeli agents to leave Britain and then kidnapped at sea. It did nothing to pacify the British MPs outraged at the suspected abuse of British law.

Secondly, by abandoning its policy of total silence on the matter, the Israeli Government unleashed a tide of recriminations and intense public debate over the security lapse that allowed Vanunu to tell his story in the first place. Israel's internal security force, the Shin Bet, already tarnished by its cover-up of the murder of two Palestinian bus hijackers, bore the brunt of the attack for its failure to act against Vanunu.

The public backlash against Vanunu threatened to spread to whole political groupings. The country's hallowed democratic traditions, the very freedoms that guaranteed Israel moral authority over the totalitarian regimes of its Arab enemies, came under fire. Refusing to believe that the Shin Bet's failings could be the result of simple incompetence, right-wing politicians in the Knesset called for a McCarthyist purge of leftist sympathisers in the security services. Criticism of the Shin Bet swamped the debate on Vanunu's kidnapping. The broad consensus that had given the Government carte blanche in its initial handling of the affair was being swept away in the demand for recriminations against political dissenters.

In the Knesset, Geula Cohen's call for a purge of the Shin Bet split the right-wing Tehiya Party. Rafael Eitan, a factional colleague of Cohen's, said in a radio interview that Cohen 'didn't mean what she said'. Eitan was summoned for a severe dressing-down by the party leader, Yuval Ne'eman.

Cohen blamed the leftists for the Shin Bet's failure to pay attention to Vanunu when he demonstrated in Beersheba alongside Arabs on behalf of a Palestinian state. Instead of stopping Vanunu, said Cohen, the leftist-infiltrated Shin Bet had encouraged him.

'Maybe the particular Shin Bet operative identified with Vanunu and would have dearly liked to demonstrate in favour of the PLO as well,' Cohen told *The*

Jerusalem Post. 'There is no other reason why questions were not asked about Vanunu's background and place of work.'

Just as leftists had infiltrated the Shin Bet at field level, she said, they were present higher up the organisation, leaking secret information to Knesset members associated with the Citizens' Rights Movement. Cohen said that Rafael Eitan was wrong to claim that a person's political views were unimportant and irrelevant to his fitness for a sensitive post.

'Anybody who preaches and works for a Palestinian State, or for dialogue with the PLO, cannot loyally promote government policy of preventing the creation of a Palestinian State,' she insisted.

Attacks by Cohen and others on the Israeli right made it clear that for many Israelis the real feeling of outrage lay less with Vanunu's nuclear revelations than with his identification with the Palestinian cause. Similarly, Vanunu's conversion to Christianity was seen by many as a more profound betrayal of the Jewish State than the act of selling his country's nuclear secrets.

In Rafel Eitan's interview on Israel Radio, he rejected Cohen's call for a purge, and scoffed at her charge that the Shin Bet had been infiltrated by leftists and PLO sympathisers. He said that nobody had ever judged the reliability of security personnel by their political viewpoints.

'That approach could prove to be a two-edged sword,' he warned. 'Today's rulers might purge holders of the opposite views, and tomorrow's rulers might purge the security men left in their jobs today, if that were the rule.'

Eitan said that 'political opinions have nothing to do with the discharge of sensitive functions', adding that believing in a Palestinian state was irrelevant in deciding a person's fitness to hold a sensitive post.

The Jerusalem Post, scarcely a bastion of liberalism, published a searing editorial on 12th November:

> Perhaps it was to be expected that Mordechai Vanunu's manifest act of treason would sooner or later encourage some right-wingers to dredge up from the political sewers the notion that left-wingers like the technician from Dimona are all a threat to national security ... until now no leading politician has ever lent his or her name to any such campaign of group vilification on the ground that 'the apple does not fall far from the tree'. The national consensus has always been that the last thing Israel needs to overcome its difficulties, both foreign and domestic, is a large dose of home-made McCarthyism.

A fortnight later, on 26th November, Benny Morris wrote an article linking Vanunu's kidnapping with Shin Bet's cover-up of the Palestinian murders and with the case of Jonathan Pollard, the US naval intelligence analyst arrested as an Israeli spy.

> To a greater or lesser degree, all Israel's non-military intelligence bodies have become 'rogue agencies' in the structural sense; that the Government—in this context the Prime Minister's Office and the Knesset—have lost control over their functioning and operations ... the spate of major security mishaps of the past two years—Pollard, the Shin Bet affair, Vanunu and, in a sense, the Iran arms affair—all demonstrate in various ways the roguery of the agencies and the loss of government control.

On the subject of Vanunu, he wrote:

> The unit of internal security responsible for sensitive in-stitutions malfunctioned. A technician with clear com-munist affiliations and strange behaviour was for years allowed to work unhampered in the Dimona nuclear reactor, to take photographs inside the reactor and to leave the country with the rolls of film. Some have described Vanunu's revelations to *The Sunday Times* as the most serious breach of Israeli security in the country's history.

The telling word 'some' in the last sentence indicated that Morris himself was not so sure. The word highlighted the dilemma faced by Israeli commentators on the Vanunu affair. While condemning the security lapse that allowed Vanunu to tell his story, Morris, like others, was openly sceptical of the real damage done by the revelations. In fact, as had already been widely pointed out, Israel stood to benefit significantly from Vanunu's actions. Israel could afford to be publicly outraged by the security breach, while secretly celebrating the prestige it won by the disclosure of its military strength, and the embarrassment that would be caused to its Arab enemies by the knowledge that Israel could not be beaten in a conventional war. It was this contradiction that stifled the nuclear debate in Israel before it had begun. Nuclear weapons were a perennial non-issue in the Israeli press and Mordechai Vanunu's revelations in themselves did little to change that.

Far more important was the international reaction to Vanunu's kidnapping, and the rumours that Israeli agents had broken foreign laws to bring him to trial. The charge that the then Prime Minister Peres had sought and gained Mrs Thatcher's consent for the kidnapping was still getting wide coverage in the British press.

On 10th November, the day after Israel admitted it was holding Vanunu, *The Daily Telegraph* quoted 'sources close to the Israeli Government' insisting that Peres phoned Mrs Thatcher on 21st September—a fortnight before *The Sunday Times* story was published—after a meeting with his Cabinet. The outcome of that meeting had been the decision to launch a Mossad operation to get Vanunu back to Israel.

Peres allegedly convinced Thatcher that Vanunu had to be punished in Israel. Thatcher was said to have agreed to tell MI6, the British intelligence service, to turn a blind eye to the Israeli action. The story of Vanunu's kidnapping came hard on the heels of the so-called 'Dikko affair', in which a former Nigerian government minister, Alhaji Umaru Dikko, was found drugged and bound inside a wooden crate at Stanstead Airport, thirty miles from London, waiting to be shipped back to Nigeria to face charges of embezzling millions of dollars from rice imports. In another crate, police had found two unbound and conscious Israelis, believed by British intelligence to have been Mossad agents. Both crates were addressed from the Nigerian High Commission to the country's Minister of External Affairs, although they were not labelled diplomatic baggage. The Dikko affair, which happened only a year after a gunman in the Libyan Embassy had killed a policewoman from inside the embassy compound, had provoked a diplomatic row with Nigeria, and prompted questions over Israel's role in the plot. Now, less than six months later, Israeli agents were once again implicated in the parcelling up of a foreign citizen to face criminal charges overseas. The House of Commons was indignant.

Two Conservative MPs, Anthony Beaumont-Dark and Dennis Waters, called for a full investigation of the circumstances surrounding Vanunu's disappearance, and the flourishing rumour that Vanunu had been shipped out of Britain in a diplomatic crate. Whitehall stalled. Although there was no official record of Vanunu having left Britain, Whitehall said this did not prove that he had been taken out of the country illegally. The Home Office system of records was far from complete, Whitehall officials said, and a tourist from outside the EC was capable of leaving the country without that fact showing up on computer records.

While Whitehall officials struggled to defend the Government's claim of ignorance, Israeli politicians expressed amazement at Thatcher's problems. In Israel the question of how Vanunu had been brought back was not seen as important. With public opinion strongly behind it in prosecuting Vanunu, the Israeli Government was chiefly concerned with placating its allies in Europe.

In Britain's case, this was proving difficult. While Mrs Thatcher fended off calls for an inquiry, the Foreign Office asked the Israeli Government to clarify its statement. The British Ambassador in Tel Aviv, William Squire, asked for clarification that Vanunu had not been kidnapped from Britain. A flimsy story then appeared in the British press naming 'Cindy' as the woman agent who lured Vanunu out to sea. This, together with Israel's reiterated assurance that it had not broken British law in getting Vanunu out of Britain, effectively killed speculation that Vanunu had been smuggled out of the country in diplomatic baggage, and took the pressure off Whitehall to come up with anything better. Satisfied by the assurance that British law had not been broken, the Thatcher Government seized on the fact that the case was now *sub judice* as an excuse for dropping the subject completely. With British police reportedly on the lookout for a 'blonde, plump and American woman' called Cindy, the matter slipped quietly off the front pages, and Whitehall was able to back away from an unwanted confrontation with the Israeli Government.

The Israeli assurance, as far as it went, was true. Mordechai Vanunu had boarded British Airways flight BA504 of his own free will. At that stage he could still have turned back. But the moment he stepped out of the terminal at Rome's Leonardo da Vinci Airport, Vanunu was in the power of the Mossad.

Cindy flagged down a nearby car and Vanunu, believing it to be an unmarked taxi, got in. Heading straight for the autostrada, the car drove away quickly in the direction of Rome. By now, Vanunu was growing suspicious. There were only three of them in the car, and it was getting dark outside. Vanunu had no idea where he was being taken, and realised how completely he had entrusted himself to two people he hardly knew. Apparently he even thought of throwing himself from the moving car, but didn't. Finally the car drew up outside a bleak apartment block just outside Rome. Vanunu got out of the car with Cindy, and followed her to the door of the apartment blocks. Cindy pulled a key out of her pocket and Vanunu followed her inside. Before Vanunu had a chance to defend himself, he was jumped on by several Mossad agents who had been waiting for him inside the apartment. Vanunu could only watch helplessly as Cindy produced a syringe and injected him with a strong sedative.

A trail of circumstantial evidence left behind by the Israeli agents showed what happened next. Almost certainly, a light-coloured van was waiting outside the apartment block at the time that Vanunu was overpowered and drugged. The van had been hired by a member of the Israeli embassy staff in Rome on the day that Vanunu had disappeared from London. For four days the Israeli agents kept Vanunu sedated and out of sight. Some time between 30th September and 4th October, the Israeli agents bundled Vanunu into the hired van and drove to the port of La Spezia, about 425 kilometres from Rome. The light-coloured van was driven back to Rome and returned to the hire company. The figure on the clock was 900 kilometres, just 50 kilometres more than the return trip from Rome to La Spezia.

On 4th October an Israeli cargo ship, the 11,000 tonne 'Tapuz', put into La Spezia. The 'Tapuz' was part-owned by Zim, the Israeli national shipping line. The captain told the harbour authorities that the ship had come from Haifa in Israel, and was bound for Marseilles. In fact, it had sailed from Barcelona. The 'Tapuz' stayed at La Spezia just long enough for the Mossad to smuggle Vanunu on board. Although the 'Tapuz' was then the only ship in La Spezia, this would not have been difficult. A port has none of the sophisticated security apparatus found at an airport. There was little in the way of security at La Spezia to get in the way of the Israelis.

Just four hours after it docked, the 'Tapuz' put to sea again. By the time the sedatives wore off, Vanunu was already far out in the Mediterranean, bound in heavy iron chains in the hold. The next time the 'Tapuz' was seen was when it put in at Ashdod in Israel, on 9th October. The crossing, which would normally take three days, had taken almost double that.

CHAPTER TEN

MOVED FROM PRISON TO PRISON during the weeks after his abduction, Vanunu ended up in Ashkelon, not far from Jerusalem. For two months nothing new was heard about the kidnapping. Rumours flourished, and bits of the truth found their way into various media fables. The real role and identity of Cindy continued to elude journalists.

Throughout this time, Vanunu remained in strictly enforced solitary confinement. Although his lawyer had access to him within days of his imprisonment, it was two months before he was allowed a visit from his family. The prison authorities built special tunnels and blacked out windows in their determination to prevent him passing on the details of his kidnapping to anyone who might leak it to the outside world. They even forced Vanunu to grow a beard so that he would be harder to identify. Vanunu's lawyer was Amnon Zichroni, a prominent human rights activist. Zichroni was the only person allowed to speak to Vanunu without a security guard standing by, but risked jail himself for passing on secret information.

Ashkelon Prison is a grey concrete box behind a high barbed-wire fence. Armed guards lounge indolently in the watchtowers, gazing at the scrub and the handful of stunted palm trees and metal grilles buried in the prison walls. A few cars are parked in the dust inside the barbed wire. Inside the prison, Vanunu was placed in a cell two metres by three metres wide by three metres high. The cell had no window, but a fluorescent lamp burned all day and night. He was constantly watched by video camera. In the cell was a small alcove with basic toilet facilities, a bed, and a few books Zichroni had brought for him. Vanunu asked especially for books by Kierkegaard. Vanunu was imprisoned under a false name, David Enosh, and his presence was kept hidden from other prisoners. Only two people in Ashkelon—one warder and the jail commandant—came into contact with him.

Martyrdom had never been part of Vanunu's plan, but at the back of his mind was the expectation that he would be punished. He had told friends in Australia that he was prepared to risk jail for what he was doing. Vanunu knew he was technically breaking the law, but he trusted people to respect his motives. He believed he could not be condemned for actions he viewed as purely moral.

But with no chance to explain himself, and facing a hostile Jewish press, Vanunu's case was portrayed within Israel as a straightforward case of treason. The media image of him as mentally unbalanced, strenuously promoted by the Israeli Government, and his feckless decision to accept money for his story, ruled out any serious examination of Vanunu's reasons for doing what he did.

The Israeli press relentlessly attacked Vanunu's character and ignored his motives. Typical of these attacks was a long article by Abraham Rabinovich, published by *The Jerusalem Post* on 14th November 1986, three days after the Government announced that Vanunu was back in Israel.

Mordechai Vanunu, one of society's invisible men, said 'notice me' last year when he posed nude for an art class at Ben-Gurion University.

He said it again when, in a brief space of time, he turned Communist, turned Christian, became an advocate of the Palestinian cause, went into voluntary exile and was arrested for selling his country's nuclear secrets.

A study of this man has less to do with splitting of atoms or divided loyalties than with a sundered personality desperately seeking fusion with its missing parts.

Rabinovich's article went on to build a picture of Vanunu's character through interviews with former high-school classmates, army mates and university acquaintances 'almost none of whom described himself or herself as a friend'. The tone of the article was established before the witnesses had even been called. In fact Vanunu, though he dabbled with communism at university, never called himself a communist. Communism was ultimately irreconcilable with the spiritual quest that Vanunu had been pursuing through his reading of Kierkegaard, and which had been weighing on him since his adolescence. Details such as this were easily swept aside in the tide of popular anger and revulsion at his perceived treachery. Vanunu's father, the elderly and austere rabbi, was quoted by Israeli newspapers as having disowned his son and closed his stall at Beersheba markets after being pelted with rotten vegetables. Vanunus all over the Negev region were reported to be changing their names to avoid being associated with the traitor.

Newspaper reports and government statements strove to demonstrate that Vanunu was mentally unstable. 'The nuclear renegade,' wrote Rabinovich, 'was himself betrayed some time in his youth by forces in life too great for him to handle.'

But Vanunu's dissatisfaction since the age of sixteen

with his Jewish upbringing, as well as the consistency of his political views, show that he was far from unstable. Instead, Vanunu's decision to reveal the secrets of Dimona was a logical and inevitable extension of his long-held oppositon to Israeli militarism and his conviction that nuclear weapons were both evil and dangerous. Grafting his moral and political beliefs onto Kierkegaard's doctrine of individual action and responsibility, Vanunu saw clearly what he had to do. He spelled out his position in a letter to an Israeli journalist, Yael Lotan, which he wrote shortly before his trial in August 1987, and which was passed on to *The Guardian* newspaper in London.

> An act like mine teaches citizens that their own reasoning is no less important than that of their leaders. Don't follow them blindly on crucial issues like nuclear weapons. If there is a case which calls for civil disobedience, it is this.
>
> Such an act undermines general confidence in the leaders. We saw that in the Lebanon war. Most people supported the war and today this has been reversed. The majority know now that it was not a war but simply bloodshed caused by a few leaders who wanted to 'impose order' in a neighbouring country by the use of force.
>
> I knew the truth from the first day of that war. I wouldn't buy the announcements of the Israeli Government and I developed a general criticism, including what is being done in the nuclear field in this country. I had to overcome many personal barriers to do what I did. The chief barrier was the sacrifice of my private life to exposure and slander, and of my future plans, on this altar.

Once in jail, Vanunu embarked on a series of protests to improve his conditions, and to complain about the way his private life had been splashed across the Israeli media. For two nights running, Israeli television broadcasted extracts from Vanunu's private diary. The Civil Rights Association accused the Israel Broadcasting

Authority of a gross invasion of privacy. Uri Porat, the Director-General of the authority, countered that 'Vanunu is not in the realm of the "right to privacy" anymore', insisting that the public had a right to know 'anything that might illuminate Vanunu's motives'. It was a flagrant breach of the very principle of *sub judice* that the Israeli Government had invoked to defend its refusal to give details of Vanunu's kidnapping.

Vanunu's lawyer, Zichroni, told the press that Vanunu was 'incensed' by the publicising of his diaries, but had left it to him to decide whether or not to sue.

On 18th November, Zichroni announced that he was meeting Justice Ministry officials to discuss the legal proceedings against Vanunu. Zichroni confirmed that he had flown to Britain and that 'certain scientists' had agreed to testify at the trial that Vanunu was acting for ideological and not financial reasons when he agreed to reveal Israel's nuclear secrets to *The Sunday Times*. Section 94 of Israel's penal code, which is included in the chapter on treason and espionage, states that 'an act shall not be regarded as an offence under this chapter if it has been done in good faith with intent to bring about, by lawful means, a change in the structure of the State or the activities of any of its authorities.'

The charges against Vanunu were filed with the Jerusalem District Court on 28th November 1986. The charge sheet acused Vanunu of 'assistance to an enemy in war' and of 'aggravated espionage'. It was signed by Israel's Attorney-General, Yosef Harish. Although the first charge carried the penalty of life imprisonment or the death sentence, section 96 stated that 'notwithstanding anything provided in this chapter, a court shall not impose the death penalty unless the offence was committed in a period in which armed hostilities were carried on by or against Israel'.

Vanunu's court appearance before Judge Zvi Cohen

was organised under heavy secrecy. The case was listed in Hebrew as 'Attorney-General vs. X'. On 30th November, with scores of journalists jostling for a view of Vanunu, a white van sped through the narrow driveway leading to the Jerusalem District Court, and pulled up outside the back entrance of the courthouse. Vanunu, wearing blue jeans, a red T-shirt, a khaki coat and tennis shoes, his features obscured by the heavy beard he had been forced to grow in prison, was bundled out of the van and through the door of the building, while flash bulbs fired all around him.

Inside the court, Judge Cohen granted Zichroni's request that the hearing be postponed, and ordered that Vanunu remain in custody. To nobody's surprise, Zichroni's appeal for an open trial was turned down. Despite the continued refusal of the prison authorities to allow a visit by his family, Vanunu's letters showed him in relatively good spirits. Exactly a week after his court appearance, he wrote to McKnight:

> I want to thank you for all that you did for me. I heard you came to Israel to see me. I hope next time you can see me. I want to say to all the people of St John's Church that I have good memories of the time I was in Sydney. I was happy to be a part of a big family. I thank God and thank you for helping me. Now I am here in the jail. I am OK waiting for the trial. I pray that they will understand me, so I don't know how long I'll be in the jail.... I have plenty of time, and I read the Bible and other books, listen to classical music and the BBC. I want to read more books about Christianity and the Anglican Church and Kierkegaard. It is not easy to be a Christian here.

Vanunu asked McKnight to arrange for an Anglican priest to visit him in prison, and finished with a quotation from Isaiah 58:6—'Is not this the kind of fasting I have chosen: to loose the chains of injustice and untie the cords of the yoke, to set the oppressed free and break every yoke?'

The day before, the Israeli press had reported a story in the London *Financial Times* alleging that Vanunu had been drugged and kidnapped en route from London to Paris, and had been flown to Tel Aviv aboard an El Al Boeing 767. He was being held in Ashkelon prison under a false name, *The Financial Times* said, and was only allowed to exercise when no other prisoners were about. The rumour that he had been abducted during a long sea voyage was reported to be a deliberate piece of disinformation put out by the Mossad to conceal the date of his arrival. In fact, the paper said, Vanunu had been undergoing interrogation for more than two months, which was not far from the truth.

Two months after being kidnapped, Vanunu was allowed a visit from his family. His brothers Danny and Albert, and his sister Bruria, spent forty-five minutes with him under the gaze of a prison officer. His parents did not come.

Although Zichroni could still visit him freely, Vanunu was now isolated from everyone else. He grew increasingly demoralised by the fierce campaign being conducted against him by the media. Shocked and affronted by the slurs on his character, he was also angry at the way the Government had stifled the facts of his arrest. Failing to grasp the power and momentum of political necessity unleashed against him, Vanunu felt that the illegality of his kidnapping robbed Israel of any right to try him, and believed that people outside, if they only knew, would share this view.

CHAPTER ELEVEN

I T TOOK ONLY SECONDS FOR VANUNU TO SHATTER THE SECRET of his abduction. The incident happened on 21st December, just as Vanunu was approaching the Jerusalem District Court to hear Judge Zvi Cohen grant the State's request that his remand be extended until the end of his trial. Vanunu, paler and thinner than he had looked at his last court appearance three weeks before, was driven to the rear entrance in a police van. Reporters again crowded around the courthouse. As the van rolled into the driveway, Vanunu suddenly leant over and pressed his palm against one of the windows of the van. Israeli and foreign media teams bustled to get closer to the van. It was over so quickly that reporters who were part of the mêlée did not even know what had happened. Before prison guards had dragged Vanunu's hand away from the window, scores of photographs had been taken. On his hand Vanunu had scribbled a message in English. The message said: 'Vanunu M WAS HIJACKEN IN ROME ITL, 30.9.86 21.00, Came to Rome BY BA FLY 504.'

Inside the court building, the message was washed off Vanunu's palm. When he re-emerged after the three-hour hearing, his handcuffed hands were pinned down by guards. But as the van worked its way through the narrow alley outside the courthouse, one of the reporters shouted a question to Vanunu in Hebrew about how he was brought back to Israel. Vanunu shouted out one word —'Rome'—before being violently muzzled by his guards.

Although the story was reported by Israeli newspapers, the message and Vanunu's shouted response were censored. Photographs showing Vanunu's hand against the window carried a black smudge across his palm. In a vain effort to prevent the information from getting out, the military censor had slapped a ban on local newspapers from revealing the words, although these were already being cabled around the world. Guards frantically tried to round up film of the incident, and warned foreign journalists of the penalties of transmitting the news from inside Israel. But within hours, *The London Evening Standard* had published the story, followed by the BBC and then by news media all over the world. Finally the censor gave up, and the message was printed in Israeli newspapers. Israeli newspapers railed against the blundering attempt by the military censor to kill the story. *The Jerusalem Post*, with wry but judicious understatement, commented that 'judging from the message Vanunu seems to have been unaware of how he reached Israel from Italy'.

The punishment for Vanunu was swift. He lost his Walkman radio, his books and the daily newspaper provided by the prisons service.

In an editorial two days after the hand message, *The Jerusalem Post* declared that the handling of the Vanunu affair had badly tarnished the military censor:

For when suppression of news is obviously not possible, to try to do so only discredits the Censor, and discredits those, in this case the Israeli press, enjoined to co-operate in such inanity.... Responsibility for Vanunu's manoeuvre rests with those delegated by the courts to shield him from public view. If they fumble, it is not for the Censor to undo what cannot be undone.

Having denounced Vanunu for disclosing his country's secrets, it was ironic to find the Israeli press now denouncing the censor for protecting them.

The international reaction was immediate, and threatened briefly to drop the Israeli Government into a diplomatic crisis as bad as the one it had recently patched up with Britain. This time the offended party was Italy.

Italy, which had created a diplomatic storm of its own when it released the Arab hijackers of the 'Achille Lauro' cruise ship, was in no position to be outraged by the behaviour of the Mossad. Italy's ambassador in Israel, Giovanni Domenido, cautiously stated that Italian law would have been broken if Vanunu had been abducted 'with violence'. Domenido said that for the moment he did not know what had happened, and would have to wait for instructions from Rome. He reminded the Israelis that the alleged kidnapping was uncomfortably reminiscent of a plot by the Egyptian secret service to kidnap an agent in a diplomatic crate from Rome. That incident had triggered a major diplomatic incident, Domenido warned.

Israel's response was a characteristic one. The Israeli Embassy in Rome said it knew nothing about the supposed abduction. The Italian Government, however, soon ordered a full police inquiry into Vanunu's disappearance. Two parliamentary deputies complained about the 'apparent impunities with which foreign intelligence forces act on Italian soil'. The kidnapping made a mockery of the recent agreement on the exchange of intelligence signed by Italy and Israel only a month before.

As a result of the palm message, Vanunu's police guards devised an elaborate way of keeping him away from the press on his next visit before the judge. For his next appearance, Vanunu was brought to the court at 5 am, an hour before the first journalists showed up for their vigil. At 7.20 am, a police van with its windows painted white drove to the back of the courthouse. A man was pulled from the van and immediately engulfed by the crowd of security men guarding the entrance.

The hearing took place in a sealed-off courtroom on the third floor. At 10.20 am, a figure emerged from the rear entrance, surrounded by security men and hidden beneath a red umbrella and a burlap sheet. The figure was pushed into the van with the whitewashed windows, and driven off in a convoy with wailing sirens. At the same time, a police car stopped at a side entrance, picked up a passenger and sped off. Nobody could tell which was Vanunu, but it was a good bet that the scene with the umbrella and sheet was a hoax to divert attention from Vanunu's quiet departure from the side entrance.

Although Vanunu had been allowed visits from his family, the confiscation of his Walkman, books and newspapers was a severe loss. It gave him a focus for his most defiant protest yet. On 4th January, during his first visit from his parents and his brother Asher, Vanunu declared that he was going on 'hungry strike'. He gave his reasons in a letter to John McKnight. In between the razor cuts of the prison censor, Vanunu wrote:

I declare a strike time. Stopped eating from 4.1.87. My [word illegible] is that they have to release me from the prison. What happened to me is against the human rights. Now they have the choice to release me or to let me die in the prison. You, as me brothers and sisters, I am asking you to do all that you can for helping my release from the prison.

Vanunu was now cut off from every aspect of the outside world. Vanunu's world was his cell, with its permanent artificial light and its video camera. The intransigence of the prison authorities threw him back more than ever on the support of McKnight and his friends at St John's:

> You, Father John, you knew why I flew to London. I am not allowed to write even if it is good or bad. I hope that the judges will believe me and understand me. So you can write letters to any governments and organisations who can help me and you can explain all the story. If they will let me go, it's a victory for human rights, a victory for freedom.

Zichroni fought vigorously for the return of Vanunu's possessions. He got a psychiatrist, Dr Ruhama Maraton, to prepare a report on Vanunu's mental condition. Maraton, though forbidden to see Vanunu, argued that depriving him of 'outside stimulants' meant that he might seek 'artificial stimulants' and injure himself through cuts, burns or a hunger strike. Appearing in open court before Judge Cohen, Zichroni's office said that Vanunu needed his radio and books to maintain his sanity. Zichroni was successful. Vanunu got back his books and radio, although the judge upheld the right of the prison warder to deny him a newspaper, since he did not pay for it himself. Vanunu, however, continued his hunger strike.

His brother Asher quoted him as saying that 'a man cannot be so lonely' and that 'my food is given to me as if I was a dog. I don't need their food'. As his hunger strike stretched into its third week, with Vanunu losing a lot of weight through his diet of tea and water, his family tried to talk him into giving up. A prison doctor was examining him daily and said his health was not at risk. The prison authorities suddenly decided to let Vanunu have one of the letters which were being sent to him in prison. Vanunu wrote back to McKnight:

I received your letter. It is a great support and encouragement in my faith. Yet they didn't allow any priest to see me.
I need him because I am alone in my faith, and also my
family didn't understand me, but I am not going to give up.
Now I'll try by the court to force them to organise the visit.
... This is my twenty-fourth day in my strike. I want that
all the world will know how they brought me to here, and
what I wanted to do.

Vanunu had petitioned the authorities to allow contact visits from his girlfriend, Judy Zimmet, who was
living in Boston. In the last week of January his plea
was turned down. Vanunu interpreted it as another
attack on his religion. He told McKnight he wanted to
marry Zimmet. Religion had nothing to do with the
decision to refuse Vanunu a contact visit from Judy
Zimmet. The State Attorney was convinced that Vanunu
would use a visit from Zimmet to pass on more secrets.
Vanunu was offered a visit, but only on condition that
the couple faced each other through a soundproof glass
screen. They were not allowed to speak but could communicate with handwritten messages which had to be
cleared by a security guard. Vanunu would not accept
the conditions. He demanded that the two be allowed to
speak over the telephone. He continued his hunger
strike and added to his list of official requests a visit
from an Anglican clergyman and an end to his solitary
confinement.

The State Attorney's office was convinced that Vanunu
would stop at nothing in his efforts to reveal more
secrets. Arguing against his demand for a visit from a
clergyman, the State said that on 1st February he had
once again tried to pass on secret information. It did not
specify to whom, but his visitors that day were his three
brothers.

Judge Cohen turned down all four requests, and on
the thirty-fourth day of his hunger strike, Vanunu gave

up, telling Zichroni he needed to build up his strength for his trial, which was expected to begin soon. Ironically, it was about to be set back by several months as a direct consequence of the arrival in Israel of Vanunu's brother Meir, an outspoken left-wing activist. With the rest of the family saying little, and the press losing interest, Meir flew from his home in Boston to stir up the issue and give his own account of his brother's motives.

'They've made him out to be public enemy No. 1,' he told reporters.

He's been portrayed as dumb, a money-grabber, basically unstable. The newspapers have played into the hands of the Shin Bet, which has led an organised campaign of incitement against Motti. Now anybody who considers himself half a patriot wants to see him hang. Motti was never interested in money. He could have got much more, plus security, if he had gone to a hostile government. They said he was a fool, but he amazed professors abroad who couldn't understand how a lowly technician could know so much about nuclear processes. He finished university, even though most of his time was taken up with political activities for the underprivileged.

Meir descibed his brother as 'an idealist ... he couldn't bring himself to harm a fly. He has always been a man of conscience.... A book on nuclear deterrence as a rallying point for doves made a big impression on him. This, and the Lebanon war, prompted Motti to act.'

With his brother Asher, who had been living in Holland, and numerous well-known left-wing activists, Meir set about attacking the Government, the prison service and the media for its treatment of Vanunu. He attacked the 'public lynch atmosphere' which had 'tried, convicted and sentenced' his brother. 'Many people think that he is worse than a Nazi war criminal,' he said.

The arrival of Meir did more than antagonise the

Israeli Government. It distorted the reasons behind Vanunu's actions. Meir hijacked his brother's cause and detached it from its most important element—his Christian faith. Vanunu had never been, nor did he want to be, a spokesman for the Left or for any other political faction. In revealing the secrets of Dimona, Vanunu had been appealing to something more than political allegiance, to a sense of individual conscience and morality. He acted because he felt God had called on him to act, not because he was bound to any political ideology. The deeper he immersed himself in his Christian faith, the less he felt able to trust those who had rallied round him for political reasons, no matter how strong their support.

With only weeks to go before the start of Vanunu's trial, Meir contrived to split the relationship between his brother and Zichroni. On 8th March, Vanunu dismissed Zichroni. The sacking was Meir's work, but the deteriorating relations between Meir and Zichroni made his departure from the case inevitable. While Meir had pressed for a line of defence based on Vanunu's supposed political motives, Zichroni had all along preferred to concentrate on the legal aspects of the trial. Though a famous human rights activist and champion of left-wing causes (he had been recommended independently to both McKnight and *The Sunday Times* as the most suitable lawyer for the job), Zichroni was opposed to turning Vanunu's case into a left-wing cause célèbre. With Meir in Israel, Zichroni found it increasingly hard to hold Vanunu's trust. After the sacking, Vanunu thanked Zichroni for his professional help, but evidently felt that he had not fought vigorously enough for improved prison conditions. Zichroni himself drily reported that Vanunu 'was not pleased by what he termed the intimate relationship I have with members of the Shin Bet'.

The account Vanunu gives in his letters suggests that his reasons had more to do with their religious differences. In a letter dated 17th March 1987, Vanunu wrote:

> One of the reasons I dismissed my lawyer is that he didn't do anything in this case of my faith. I wrote by myself an appeal to the court to meet a priest.

Meir, too, suspected that Zichroni may have been working on a plea bargain to reduce Vanunu's charge from treason to the less serious one of espionage. Zichroni denied this. Meir now concedes that his suspicion was based on nothing more than rumour. There was, however, another reason behind his decision to get rid of Zichroni. Meir believed that Zichroni was intent on getting the trial over as quickly as possible, and that this would rule out any serious public discussion of the case. He wanted to replace Zichroni with someone who would stir up the political debate surrounding the trial, and who would fight the Israeli Government over its determination to keep the trial secret.

What seems certain is that Zichroni's failure to share the same religious values as Vanunu, and to fully understand the importance Vanunu placed on his Christian faith, opened a rift which Meir's arrival merely widened. On 4th April he wrote to McKnight:

> I hope you received my letters to you. I haven't received any letter from you. My brother said to me you had talked with him and you sent four letters. Maybe your letters to me are in Amnon's [Zichroni's] hands and he didn't give them to me. He is not my lawyer any more. I find that he works against me all the time. I didn't know him well. I asked him to do many things, to provide for the trial, and he did not do them. So I decided with my brother Meir to take someone else. I hope he, the new lawyer, will be better. The trial will be a few months later.... I can't phone from here. I cannot write about my motives, why I published the information, because they do not want the people to know the truth.

They want to put me as a spy, a communist, a criminal. That is what the newspapers wrote here. In all this my lawyer Amnon does not help me. He plays like he is one of the government people.

In another letter, a month later, Vanunu said that Zichroni 'doesn't help to release my case. I felt that he with the prosecution wanted to launch my trial very fast and to send me for a long time to jail.'

The dismissal of Zichroni set the trial back many months, and allowed Meir to concentrate attention on the political aspect of Vanunu's case. It also marked the first stage in a process of disengagement with the outside, political, Jewish world which ended with Vanunu cutting himself off from everyone who could not share his Christian faith.

Mistrustful of the political activists who had taken up his cause, Vanunu depended on McKnight and his friends at St John's Church for support and understanding. A month after sacking Zichroni, he told McKnight:

They know that you are my father in faith, and that you and St John's parish know me very well. So they believe by separating me from you I'll be here alone, as a criminal, a spy that all the people hate here. I am now suffering for my religious belief. For me, now is the real life. Now I am carrying my cross.

In his first weeks in prison, Vanunu had entrusted everything to Zichroni, directing McKnight to write to him via Zichroni, and asking McKnight to arrange for an Anglican priest to contact Zichroni. Now he accused Zichroni of conspiring with the prison authorities to hold back his letters: 'I know you sent me the letters,' he wrote, 'but they and Amnon didn't want to give them to me. They want to separate me from you, from my Lord Jesus Christ, but they will not succeed.'

In fact it was not Amnon Zichroni, but the prison

authorities which had delayed and prevented mail from reaching Vanunu. They had done so ever since his arrival, and continued to do so despite his protests. Since Vanunu's mail was always strictly checked by the prison censor, these letters were clearly not a security risk. Withholding them was part of a calculated campaign to demoralise him. It therefore served a similar purpose to the rigorous conditions of his solitary confinement, about which Vanunu never ceased to complain.

Meir and Asher Vanunu continued to recruit activists from a range of left-wing groupings to protest on Vanunu's behalf. An Israeli journalist, Yael Lotan, to whom Vanunu had been writing from prison, and who was about to face trial concerning a meeting she had had with PLO officials in Romania, joined Meir and Asher in publicly calling for an open trial. 'Otherwise we will have Star Chamber proceedings here and Vanunu will be like the Man in the Iron Mask.'

Mani Barzilai, a member of the East for Peace organisation, appropriated an argument that had been voiced by those with diametrically opposed political beliefs when he declared that Vanunu had made a 'significant contribution to Israel's security'. He said that a poll conducted in Jerusalem by his organisation revealed that 'a large number of Jews of Muslim-country origin admire Vanunu and do not think of him as a traitor'. The news that Jews arriving from enemy Arab territory did not see Vanunu as a traitor was hardly likely to find sympathy among conservative Israelis.

Another journalist, Haim Baram, attacked what he called the 'collaborationist Editors' Committee' which, he said, was 'capitulating to the pro-nuclear lobby headed by Shimon Peres'. After dismissing Amnon Zichroni, Vanunu needed a new lawyer. The man he chose was Avigdor Feldman, another prominent civil rights activist. Vanunu, with the almost childlike optimism that he had shown since his imprisonment, wrote to McKnight on 10th April that 'I am waiting for a new lawyer and if he will work very good I can be free very soon.'

On 2nd May, he wrote:

My new lawyer is Feldman. I hope he will do good work. He is a good man and he works with another lawyer. My case is difficult for me because the Government is part of this case and they want to put me for a long time in jail. Then no-one will know about what they do, and what is the truth. Now most of the people here, they do not believe me and they think about me as a spy. I am in a very bad situation and my hope is that God will help me and that the Justices will judge me by the just way.

Vanunu's petition for visits from an Anglican priest had been turned down in court. Deprived of contact with anyone except his lawyer, Vanunu fell back deeper and deeper into himself and his Christian faith. He repeatedly asked for books on Kierkegaard. His letters endlessly reaffirmed his belief that he had done God's will and that God would provide for him.

The Anglican Church, meanwhile, was less forthcoming. In February, the Anglican Church in Israel was reported to be denying any interest in Vanunu's case. A source said to be 'close to the Episcopal Church of Jerusalem and the Middle East' was quoted as saying, 'We have no connection with this man', and as denying that the Church had received any request to visit Vanunu in Ashkelon. The Church had its base at St George's Cathedral in East Jerusalem, where John McKnight had met several Anglican clergymen during his stay in Israel. It was now saying that it had no proof that Vanunu had ever been converted to Christianity. Other Christian figures contacted by Israeli reporters voiced scepticism over Vanunu's conversion, but one, the Revd Michael Bullman of the Israel Trust of the Anglican Church, said that anybody asking for a pastoral visit would have their request considered by the Church. All stressed their refusal to get involved in the legal and moral question of Vanunu's actions.

Even in St John's Church, Darlinghurst, where Vanunu had been converted to Christianity, there were some who objected to McKnight's campaigning on Vanunu's behalf. There was concern from the newer parishioners over Vanunu's actions. Several had strong Zionist sympathies. One incident was typical. McKnight had put a rectangle of tape the dimensions of Vanunu's cell (3 metres by 2 metres) on the carpet of the chancel at St John's. It provoked much comment, and was torn up one day while McKnight was away overseas. The reason given was that people found it too 'disturbing'. Vanunu himself was unaware of any such divisions, imagining that the church and all his friends there would remain just as he had left them. On the anniversary of his arrival at St John's, he wrote: 'A year ago 23.5.86 I took my first step to St John's Church. I want to say thank you, my Lord, and you whom I met on the first night, with David, Gill, Simon, Billy. God bless you. This event, it is a very very important one in my life. One day we will meet again.'

Meanwhile Amnesty International, the London-based human rights organisation, said it was concerned that media coverage of Vanunu's case would damage his chances of a fair trial by influencing the judges' decisions. In Australia, a group of senators nominated Vanunu for the Nobel Peace Prize. His nomination was later backed by the British-based Bertrand Russell Peace Foundation. Vanunu's nomination was supported by several prominent British writers and philosophers, including Graham Greene and Auberon Waugh. The Nobel nomination was particularly encouraging for Vanunu. 'I want to thank all the senators who signed it,' he wrote. 'My honour is your honour and their honour, and all this activity is improving the knowledge of nuclear weapons in all the world.'

But international support for Vanunu's actions was far from unanimous. After Vanunu had been in solitary confinement for almost six months, he suddenly became preoccupied with a bundle of letters he had received from a man called Benjamin Merhav in Melbourne. Merhav was an expatriate Israeli Jew and a committed anti-Zionist. At first he campaigned strongly for Vanunu's release, co-ordinating rallies in Melbourne by the People for Nuclear Disarmament group, and making endless reverse-charge calls to John McKnight in Sydney to discuss Vanunu's plight. In a letter dated 10th April, 1987, and left unusually intact by the censor, Vanunu wrote to McKnight:

> I cannot forget how they kidnapped me and brought me here. It is unlawful, against my will. They broke international laws. It is a terror act. It is not a democratic country, and they prevent me from saying what happened and demanding my rights. But you and all the people who care about a human being, don't be quiet. Write letters and do all that you can until they will know and understand that no one will forget what they did. One man, I don't know him, his name is Benjamin Merhav—he wrote me letters. I answered his letters, but now I am not writing him any more letters. Don't trust him and don't co-operate with him because he wrote against Christians, against the church, against you. Leave him alone.

His tirade against Benjamin Merhav was especially surprising in the light of Merhav's ardent support of Vanunu in the weeks after his disappearance. On 2nd November 1986, Australia's *National Times* newspaper had published a letter from Merhav, in which he accused the Israelis of having kidnapped Vanunu. 'As a result of this flagrant act of terrorism,' Merhav wrote, 'in open breach of international law, and in brazen violation of basic human rights, Mordechai Vanunu is now locked up in jail in Israel.'

Merhav declared that by disclosing Israel's nuclear arsenal, Vanunu had 'done a great service to humanity. He surely deserves the support and solidarity of all people of goodwill in this country of which he was a guest. Mordechai Vanunu must be immediately released from his unlawful detention—unharmed—and be able to return to his host country, Australia.'

On 2nd May, Vanunu wrote again accusing Merhav of working against him:

> They also publish in the papers that I eat kosher food. There is much disinformation, and one man trying to help them is Benjamin Merhav from Melbourne. He wrote me letters against the Anglican Church, against you, so I didn't write him any more letters. Maybe he used my letters to him—three—against me and the Christian world.

The argument between Vanunu and Merhav was the result of two clashing philosophies. Merhav, like the Israeli Left, wanted to adopt Vanunu for his own cause. But Vanunu did not share Merhav's anti-Zionist passion any more than Merhav shared Vanunu's Christianity. Merhav refused to accept Vanunu's conversion. Their falling out was inevitable. It was the first of many political and religious disagreements that would come between Vanunu and his supporters, and push him further into the solitude of his Christian faith.

Finally the prison authorities allowed Vanunu a visit from a lay Anglican, Brother Gilbert Sinden. The two men could communicate by passing notes to each other through a prison guard, and prayed together in silence. For the first time in eight months, Vanunu was allowed to receive Holy Communion. Gilbert brought him several books about Christianity and the Bible and the Anglican Church. Vanunu asked Gilbert to bring him a small cross for his cell. He also asked if he could be confirmed in prison, and told Gilbert he wanted to study theology.

CHAPTER TWELVE

TEN MONTHS AFTER VANUNU'S KIDNAPPING, the missing details of the operation were pieced together by *The Sunday Times* in a front-page story entitled 'How Israeli Agents Snatched Vanunu'. Citing 'crucial new evidence', the report described how Mossad agents had dragged Vanunu back to Israel to face trial for treason. This new evidence was allegedly obtained from Meir Vanunu, and consisted of a precise account of how his brother had been lured to Rome 'with the promise of sex'—a claim which Vanunu himself denied—and then attacked by two men, injected with a powerful anaesthetic and smuggled out of Italy on a cargo ship. Meir claimed to have personally received the kidnap story from Vanunu in jail by distracting the guard's attention. According to *The Sunday Times*, Meir decided to give his evidence despite being warned by Israeli security police that details of the kidnapping were a State secret and he could be jailed for fifteen years for revealing them.

'What I've done, I've done for my brother,' he said, in a characteristic show of bravado. 'It was my duty to tell the Italian authorities what Israel did to Mordechai. The Italian Government must protest to the Israeli

Government and do everything it can to get Mordechai back to Italy.'

Meir refused to explain precisely how he received the information. Although Vanunu's family, unlike Brother Gilbert, did not have to look at him through a sound-proof glass screen, they could only speak to him through a metal grille. A guard in the room listened to everything they said. While Meir might have succeeded in corroborating certain parts of the story, journalists expressed scepticism that he had obtained such a precise account right under the nose of a prison guard. The only people who had been allowed unrestricted access to Vanunu were his lawyers, Amnon Zichroni and Avigdor Feldman, and they were forbidden from passing on anything that related to the kidnapping. Meir was content to leave his true source discreetly hidden, saying only that the information had come from his brother.

It was, however, useful to the Israeli authorities to support the pretence that Meir had received the story directly from Vanunu, since this strengthened its case for keeping Vanunu isolated. Rejecting Vanunu's request to speak to an Anglican clergyman, the State prosecutor reiterated the Government's belief that Vanunu was bent on giving away more secrets. The prosecutor submitted an affidavit by a security agent dubbed 'Boaz', who recounted a meeting in which Vanunu told his brothers about 'the place from where he was brought to Israel, the vehicle in which he was brought and the methods employed to bring him here'. Agent 'Boaz' added that Vanunu urged his brothers to have the information published by the foreign press. The Prosecutor gave no hint of how Vanunu managed to tell his story under such stringent security.

Unlike the diplomatic furore created by the earlier rumours, the response to the true story was muted. Once again, *The Sunday Times'* exclusive access to Meir gave little incentive to the Fleet Street tabloids to follow up the story. At a press conference following the story, Meir called upon Britain to protest against the kidnapping. 'I firmly believe that the British Government should intercede and declare his forthcoming trial in Israel illegal,' he said. But foreign governments were losing interest in Vanunu. The British rejected Meir Vanunu's plea for an investigation into his brother's disappearance. A government spokesman said the matter had already been thoroughly investigated and 'no evidence whatsoever' had been found to back up Meir Vanunu's claims. Declaring that Meir's account of Vanunu's kidnapping 'adds nothing to the sum of human knowledge', the spokesman left no doubt that for the Thatcher Government, at least, the case was over. Within days, Israel Radio announced that the Israeli authorities had issued a warrant for Meir's arrest. Ostensibly, the warrant was issued as a result of Meir's kidnap revelations. It was widely assumed that the real reason was to keep Meir out of Israel during his brother's impending trial.

Meir's revelations did flush out several lengthy articles in the Israeli press justifying the kidnapping while decrying the secrecy surrounding it. A certain Jeremy Weil, writing a letter to the editor of *The Jerusalem Post*, said that 'many people were proud of the efficiency of our intelligence agencies in smuggling Mordechai Vanunu back into Israel. Unfortunately, it is a story of which the whole country may yet become increasingly ashamed unless the cloak of secrecy is lifted.'

Until now, the Jerusalem District Court had barred Vanunu's lawyer, Avigdor Feldman, from mentioning the circumstances of Vanunu's capture in his defence. Feldman took his case to the Supreme Court, and won permission from Supreme Court Justice Gavriel Bach to use the facts of Vanunu's abduction, the conditions under which he was held and his mental condition at the time. Vanunu was still prevented from saying where he was taken from, where he was held or who had carried out the kidnapping. The trial was to remain secret. Feldman hoped to use Vanunu's testimony to prove that his abduction was illegal, and so have the case thrown out. The decision was an important victory for Feldman. It was based, said Bach, on the need to 'strike a balance between the interests of State security and the defendant's right to a fair trial'.

On the face of it, this was an encouraging sign. In fact, a long list of legal precedents made it extremely unlikely that it would have any effect. The most serious precedent involved the Nazi war criminal Adolf Eichmann, who was found guilty and executed despite the obvious illegality of his abduction from Argentina. Even without the Eichmann precedent, there was an established logic in Israeli law that would have counted against Vanunu. Unlike US law, which refuses to accept any evidence obtained through illegal means, Israeli law will accept reliable evidence or information even if it is obtained illegally. Vanunu's defence hinged on the judges' acceptance of the American doctrine that illegally obtained evidence poisons all other evidence obtained as a result of it—the so-called 'fruit of the poison tree theory', or exclusionary rule.

The Israeli Supreme Court had repeatedly rejected attempts to import the exclusionary rule into Israeli law. In describing the Israeli rule, the court said, 'It is an accepted and well-established rule of the Israeli legal system that evidence, which is of itself reliable and proper, but which was obtained by illegitimate and illegal means, is admissible, and that a court has no discretion to reject it.'

The Knesset, however, had enacted a version of the exclusionary rule in two statutes: the Secret Monitoring

Law, which outlawed wire-tapping and other forms of unauthorised secret monitoring, and the Protection of Privacy Law, which gave a court the qualified right to reject evidence on the ground that it was obtained by an invasion of privacy. The more serious the crime, the more likely the evidence was to be admitted.

While lawyers argued about what evidence was and was not admissible, Vanunu's condition in jail remained the same. Since March he had been writing weekly letters to McKnight. He wrote constantly about his sense of isolation and what he always called the 'unhumanbeing' conditions of his imprisonment. He returned again and again to his idea—derived jointly from the Bible and from the writings of Kierkegaard—of the responsibility of knowledge, and the danger of keeping it hidden. In one letter he wrote:

> I want to warn the world from the nuclear perils. But they [the Israeli Government] want to avoid thinking about them. But their presence among us makes us sick in all the world. The knowledge we thus gain cannot in itself protect us from nuclear annihilation, but without it we cannot begin to take the measures that can actually protect us. Whatever is hidden away will be brought out into the open, and whatever is covered up will be uncovered.

Vanunu remained defiantly optimistic about the trial. Again, he took his confidence from the Bible. 'My trial will be in September,' he wrote, 'and I believe the sentence will be very good. "For the moment when we will be saved is closer now than it was when we first believed. The night is nearly over. Day is almost here."'

Vanunu constantly referred to the conditions of his confinement, harping on the dimensions of his cell and the sameness of his daily routine with an insistence that seemed to reflect his mental retreat from the world outside.

Now I am sure that my release will be very soon because I have good lawyer, and the judges will understand what I did, will see what I want to do is for peace to warn the people. My life here every day is the same, reading and walking in the cell. I decided not to go outside until they give me human rights, so I'll stay here in my cell until my release. I am walking few hours, my cell is 2x3 metres, and I am closing my eyes and thinking about St John's Church, Sunday morning prayer, and I can see you and all my brothers shake hands and say 'peace be with you'.

As a result of his refusal to leave his cell, Vanunu's condition visibly deteriorated. His lawyer, Feldman, described him as becoming confused and disoriented by never seeing the sun. With the fluorescent light in his cell switched on for twenty-four hours a day, Vanunu never knew whether it was day or night. Feldman visited him one afternoon and found him asleep, thinking that it was the middle of the night.

As the trial approached, Vanunu stepped up his protests, urging McKnight in one letter to lobby Amnesty International and other human rights organisations on his behalf. Amnesty wrote to the Attorney General several times asking for permission to send an observer to the trial, but this was refused. Amnesty decided to send someone anyway, and a Dutch lawyer was delegated to fly to Israel to prepare a report on the way the trial was conducted. Vanunu also asked McKnight to urge the Australian senators who had nominated him for the Nobel Peace Prize to write to Amnesty. 'It does not help to write to Israel's Prime Minister,' he wrote. The censor allowed all his complaints to pass untouched.

Vanunu's protests were not confined to his letters. One day he smeared shaving cream on the lens of the closed circuit television camera in his cell. As punishment, he was barred from receiving family visits for nearly a fortnight.

Despite the belligerent and optimistic pose that he adopted in his letters, Vanunu was becoming increasingly demoralised by his isolation. He had not been allowed to have any of the many letters that had been sent to him by McKnight and his other supporters in Australia. 'Only my faith keeps me alive,' he wrote on 3rd July. Yet a fortnight later, with a firm date set for his trial, he again seemed confident of his release. He wrote:

The trial will be at 30.8.87. Now I have a good lawyer and I hope that the result of my trial will be very good. I am yet in very bad conditions—unhumanbeing, isolated. I am not allowed to meet Judy and to speak and pray with Br Gilbert, but I am in good spirit. My hope is to be free very soon and to come again to St John's Church.

At times Vanunu displayed a childlike belief in the power of his own convictions to sway the judges. He wrote to McKnight on 22nd July:

I am not worried about my trial, because I did something good for all the people. I was not a spy and I didn't work for any government or communist country. I want all the world to know the truth, the very bad truth.

On other occasions, Vanunu showed that he was fully aware of the political pressure to find him guilty. Six days after declaring that he was 'not worried' about his trial, Vanunu told McKnight:

By God's will the judges will see and understand that I wanted to warn the people from the nuclear peril, nuclear holocaust. The security services, they have been trying too many bad things, false things, so that they can succeed to send me for a long time to jail, but now I have a good lawyer, and I am very optimistic.

In the month before the trial, with only sporadic mentions of his case in the international press, Vanunu began to devote large chunks of his letters to explaining his motives. The censor cut swathes out of several letters in a row. 'They censor my motives,' Vanunu added in a plaintive footnote to the censor's heavy black scribble.

In Australia, McKnight was interviewed by *The Australian* newspaper. He said: 'Israel is in a moral bind. They executed Eichmann because he obeyed the directions of his superiors, and not the dictates of his conscience, when he killed thousands of Jews. Now they want to punish Vanunu for doing what Eichmann did not.'

The Eichmann analogy was especially pertinent in view of the trial of John Demjanjuk. In March 1986, Demjanjuk, a US car worker, had been extradited to Israel to face accusations that he was the sadistic Treblinka prison guard Ivan the Terrible. Demjanjuk's trial, which began a year later, was a show trial broadcast every evening on prime-time Israeli television. By contrast, Vanunu's trial was to be surrounded in secrecy, to the extent that certain pieces of evidence were to be withheld even from Vanunu's counsel. He wrote:

They play with my letters, and the worst that they could play with is my trial, like what they do in other secret trials. They can give false documents and lie to the judges, so it will not be easy with the security service, but no matter what they do I'll be free and I'll come again to St John's Church.

On 2nd September, Vanunu got his chance to testify in court about the way he had been brought back to Israel and the confessions he had made after his arrest. To prevent any recurrence of the hand message, he was brought to court in a van with whitewashed windows, his features almost hidden behind a full-face motorcycle helmet and the heavy beard he had been made to grow. This time he did not repeat his trick of the day before, when he tried to remove the helmet. Sirens wailed as the van emptied Vanunu into a crowd of police and border police guarding the court building on Salah a-Din Street, which had been boarded up with thick wooden planks to prevent any view of Vanunu through the windows. Locked in the sweltering heat of the airless courtroom, judges and lawyers made a vain bid to have the windows opened. Security men refused to remove the boards.

During his three-and-a-half-hour testimony in the closed courtroom, Vanunu described how the confession he gave had been affected by the circumstances of his arrest. He did not attempt to stray from the secrecy guidelines imposed on him by the Supreme Court. Avigdor Feldman described the testimony as 'calm'. He said that Vanunu was 'satisfied' that he had told the court all that he had wanted to. Security police rejected a request by Feldman to allow Vanunu's brothers Asher and Danny to see Vanunu during the recess. A meagre gathering of supporters demonstrated outside the court with banners declaring 'Motti isn't dangerous—the trial is' and 'Let my people know'. They were moved on by police, who claimed that the signs might influence the judges. Vanunu emerged from the hearing to another chorus of police sirens, and was whisked off by a different route to avoid the demonstrators hoping to shout encouragement as he left.

A week into his trial, Vanunu seemed torn between an almost euphoric confidence in his own cause, and the growing conviction that the judges were being pressured to find him guilty. He wrote:

I feel good. My spirits are high. Now after one week of the beginning of my trial everyone knows that thay cannot condemn me as a spy. [five lines censored and illegible]

about Meir you can ask the journalist Peter Hounam. He
can tell you that the Israelis came to Sydney before we left.
'Do not let anyone deceive you in any way.' I hope that
the TV program [an ABC *Four Corners* documentary on
Vanunu's disappearance] was good. My prison conditions
are the same. Isolation, and yet I cannot speak with anyone,
not Br Gilbert, not Judy. It is now almost one year. If I feel
good it is because of my faith, my belief ... the defence case
is not easy, because this case is very complicated and
the security service try to influence the judges by many
obstacles and disinformation on the news media. So it is not
going to be just ... but when I'm free, I'll say the truth about
this Jewish country.

Despite the dismal prospects in court, it was the
prison authorities' refusal to allow Vanunu to speak to
Brother Gilbert that he seemed to find most distressing.
'Next week I'll meet Br Gilbert after he come from the
USA,' he wrote a fortnight into the trial.

Again, the court decided that we cannot speak or pray
together because the security service doesn't like me to
have a priest who can give me encouragement. They want
to break my soul, my faith, so they say that I want to give
secrets to the priest and the priest will go to the enemies.
The court believes the security service. What would happen
in the world if some Jew was not allowed to see his rabbi. ...
But I am strong in my faith. I know these people here and
everyone knows about their actions in Lebanon.

Apart from occasional newspapers and the books
brought to him by Brother Gilbert and the lawyers,
nothing was allowed to reach Vanunu in prison. He
wrote often to McKnight asking for cassette recordings
of the services at St John's. McKnight sent them, but
they merely joined the piles of letters Vanunu was
prevented from seeing. Then, for no apparent reason,
the prison authorities decided at the end of September
to let Vanunu have the cassettes. The recordings of

McKnight's morning service offered Vanunu a glimpse of freedom. He wrote:

Dear Father John,
   I am very glad to hear your voice and all my brothers and my sisters of St John's parish. I received six cassettes, four of Sunday morning prayer, one from Francis [a parishioner at St John's] and one from the meeting one night before my trial, and three books. As you see, they haven't succeeded in breaking my soul and my faith. And those cassettes that you sent in February, I have received them now. Now I can close my eyes and listen to the Sunday morning prayer and forget my cell, my prison all around me and fly back to St John's and be with you. My soul is with you every Sunday and I am praying with you. I exist here and there, and I'll keep the spirit of St John's Church with me all the time until my coming back.

By now, even Vanunu could see that the trial was not going well. He interpreted the decision not to allow free visits by Judy Zimmet or Brother Gilbert as a bad sign.

The judge [District Court Judge Zvi Cohen] ... believes the security service, that I have many secrets and I'll give those to the priest and the priest will give those to the enemies. So I'll wait to see what will be in the end of the trial. Now I am not sure about the judges. Who knows what they have in their mind and if justice is important for them.

On 30th September, Vanunu again went on hunger strike, this time to mark the first anniversary of his kidnapping. The date he chose was a reminder that, in his eyes, the kidnap took place in England. 'I am in hungry strike to mark a year of the crime they acted against me. I want to tell by it that no one will forget the unlawful action against a man, against human rights and humanbeing.... I demand my justice my rights!' Later he wrote: 'This strike is all I can say and do against the evil power. This is my voice.'

Although anxious to maintain the support he was getting from outside, Vanunu had no illusions that it would bring his freedom. A letter dated 8th October reads:

All this cannot help my release. My release will be by the judges ... maybe after the trial you and the others can do more, but as I know the security service they know how to destroy any supporters for me, yet I am optimistic that I'll be free by court soon.

Such optimism was, as always, short-lived and ambiguous. 'It does not matter what will happen in the trial,' Vanunu wrote shortly afterwards. 'It is no justice. Here in this country where secret things are involved there can be no justice. My justice is Jesus.'

Sometimes Vanunu sounded confident, sometimes indifferent to what was going on in court. He withdrew deeper into the privacy of his Christian faith. The actual details of his trial often seemed of little interest to him. He was deeply depressed and demoralised by his impregnable isolation.

McKnight and his colleague from St John's, Stephen Gray, flew to Israel in November to try to see Vanunu in jail. They were turned away. For Vanunu, who only learned of their coming after they had gone, it was a bitter blow.

Dear Father John,
    I am very sad because we were not allowed to meet. You came here from Australia twice to see me, to encourage me in my struggle, but they—the security service—didn't let you. Why is not a matter of secrets, because we could meet like I am meeting Br Gilbert. But I can tell you that now I understand more their way of separating me from my brothers and sisters in Jesus Christ.

In the courthouse of the Jerusalem District Court, Avigdor Feldman was marshalling his witnesses. The defence case rested on the claim that Vanunu had revealed nothing new, and that, if anything, Israel's security had been strengthened by the revelations. Feldman also had to confront the crucial question of money, which had seriously threatened to damage Vanunu's claims to have been acting on his conscience. By calling witnesses such as Peter Hounam from *The Sunday Times*, Feldman hoped to convince the judges that Vanunu's reasons for telling his story were moral, not financial.

After months of almost universal hostility and disbelief, the arrival of friendly witnesses who publicly supported and trusted him gave Vanunu a new burst of confidence. On 10th December he wrote to McKnight:

> The trial is continuing, and Peter Hounam, Frank Barnaby gave their witnesses. Now the judges heard about my motives, about why and what I did. It looks as if they start to understand the case from my point of view. Yet we don't know what their decision is. Other witnesses will come in the next month.

The longer the trial went on, the more obsessed Vanunu became about the interference of the Shin Bet in his case. In the beginning Vanunu had been certain that the Israeli public would see through the media campaign against him. Now he began to see even his former friends and supporters as part of a Jewish conspiracy against him. The only people he felt he could trust, apart from his brothers and his lawyer, were fellow-Christians. His about-face towards the Israeli journalist, Yael Lotan, demonstrated his increasingly paranoid distrust of everything Jewish.

Yael Lotan was a strong-minded woman and an outspoken leftist. She had defended Vanunu from the outset, and had played an important role in rallying support and organising petitions for him in Israel. At the start of the trial, Vanunu had singled her out as one of the few sympathetic to his conversion. 'She is one of a few people who support me from the beginning,' he told McKnight. 'In her first letter she wrote that when she heard I had become a Christian then she understood that my motives were for the humanbeing, not as most of the newspapers wrote that I wanted money or was helping the Arab countries.'

Scarcely three months later, he was warning McKnight not to trust her.

> I am sorry to tell you that you cannot trust the people of the committee, like Gideon Spiro and Yael Lotan. I find that they are working against my Christianity, and they are not helping me. I stopped writing them letters and cut any relation with them. It is very difficult to trust people in my case because the security services are involved. So I want to tell you not to send them any money. You cannot find people here who will support my Christianity. I don't care about them, because they don't do anything to help me.

McKnight believes that Vanunu misunderstood Yael Lotan, just as he had misunderstood other non-Christians who had given their support to him. Lotan had been consistently supportive of Vanunu. She was also aware of the essentially tribal nature of Judaism. She felt that Vanunu would never be forgiven for betraying his religion. Lotan also believed that by constantly emphasising his Christianity, Vanunu would destroy his chances of a sympathetic hearing from the judges. Vanunu, as usual, was implacable. He interpreted Lotan's concern as an assault on his faith. 'Now I don't have any friends,' he wrote. 'I think it's good if you can tell my brother Meir who can help him in England, then he will not trust all the left wing. Most of them, they are spying. You can trust my lawyer and my brothers.'

In January, Vanunu abandoned his self-imposed seclusion and decided to take daily exercise in the courtyard. 'I think that for my health I have to see the sun and not stay in this small cell all the time,' he wrote, 'so after seven months I begin to get out every day.'

Exercising in the sun, while it may have improved his physical health, did not rid Vanunu of his suspicions. On 25th January, he wrote to McKnight:

> As I wrote in my last letters, my friends are only my brothers in Christ. I found that all those who say they are my friends and support me were against my Christianity, even Judy. So now I am not writing to anyone, not Yael Lotan or Judy. I am asking you do not write or co-operate with them. Don't give them any support. My friend is Br Gilbert. He is visiting me and helping me in my struggle. All that I need is to keep my faith in Jesus.

A month later, he cut himself off completely from his non-Christian friends:

> Now I don't have any friends. All those who came to help me, they came only to separate me from my faith in Jesus, even Judy. I don't know what they said to you. Now I am happy to find that they didn't want to help me. God help me and save me from my 'friends'. For my enemies, I can see them.

For a time Vanunu even turned against his own family. 'I don't write to anyone else,' he told McKnight. 'Don't trust anyone, neither Judy nor my brother Asher. All of them are against my Christianity, but God helped me to know what they did.'

Vanunu's disparagement of Judy Zimmet represented more than just an emotional separation. The reasons had little to do with Zimmet herself, but grew from Vanunu's obsessive belief that those who could not share his Christian faith were trying to destroy it. Like Yael Lotan, Zimmet had supported Vanunu regardless of his conversion. During the first months of his imprisonment, Vanunu had talked of marrying Zimmet in a Christian church. Zimmet, although she anticipated strong opposition from her staunchly Jewish parents, had still considered marrying Vanunu. She was, however, pragmatic where Vanunu had been idealistic. She found it impossible to share his naive optimism about the trial. Zimmet remained emotionally committed to the relationship, such as it was, but wanted to wait for the outcome of the trial before she made her decision. If Vanunu was to be found guilty and given a long jail sentence, Zimmet was not prepared to wait, and said so.

As Vanunu and Zimmet became gradually alienated from each other, she continued to struggle tirelessly for his release, contributing money to his campaign fund in the United States and organising rallies and speeches appealing for his release. Although the distance between them had made it impossible to keep up any meaningful relationship while Vanunu was in jail, Zimmet was badly hurt when he finally broke off their friendship. It was a symbolic break. After eighteen months in Ashkelon Prison, Vanunu had finally cut himself off completely from his Jewish past. Vanunu's mother, Mazal, continued to visit him occasionally, his five brothers and five sisters more frequently, but his father, Rabbi Solomon, almost never.

CHAPTER THIRTEEN

O N 24TH MARCH 1988, MORDECHAI VANUNU
WAS FOUND GUILTY on three counts of espionage,
treason and disclosing State secrets. Uzi Hasson,
the State prosecutor, appeared outside the Jerusalem
courthouse to face waiting reporters. Hasson announced
that Vanunu had been convicted of collecting and
delivering information with the intent of endangering
State secrets and aiding an enemy in a war against
Israel. On Sunday 27th March, the three-judge court
passed sentence. At a brief hearing, Vanunu spoke and
Avigdor Feldman submitted a petition appealing for
leniency which was signed by twenty scientists, including twelve Nobel Prize winners. The judges decided
against imposing the maximum life imprisonment
which would have amounted to twenty years, and
sentenced Vanunu to eighteen years. The detailed
explanation of the judges' verdict was sixty pages long.
It was so secret that only one sentence was made public:
'We decided the defendant is guilty on all three counts.'

Avigdor Feldman was allowed to read all sixty pages,
but was prevented by Israel's security laws from revealing any details. Feldman was convinced that there was
disagreement between the judges over whether Vanunu

was guilty of treason. 'In their reasons for the decision you can hear two different and distinct voices,' he said. He believed that the judges could not agree over Vanunu's motives for leaking the information to *The Sunday Times*. 'The judges concluded that Vanunu did not intend to assist the enemies of Israel, but they did find that he should have known his actions would do so. Therefore he was found guilty.' Feldman thought the disagreement boded well for his appeal to the Supreme Court, where there was more scope for argument on such issues.

The guilty verdict came as no surprise to Vanunu. Feldman described him as 'very disappointed', but said he had taken the verdict calmly. Vanunu saw it as merely the culmination of an unjust law which had sanctioned his kidnapping and kept him in solitary confinement. It seemed, paradoxically, to reassure him that he had done the right thing.

After hearing his sentence, Vanunu wrote to McKnight:

> Now after I have heard the sentence all I can say is that justice was not done. It was not justice.... They gave me a very long period in jail—more than others who work for the enemies or KGB. Why? It is because I did the right thing. If they did not convict me they would have to convict the Government. So this is the easy way for them and for the security service. What they did from the beginning is unlawful. Yet I'll wait to see what the Supreme Court will say. I believe that there the judges will be more free from government influence ... the most important thing is that I chose to do what I did and I believe that I did the right thing, and I didn't break the law. The Government broke the law and the day will come when this Government will say the truth to their people about the nuclear issue.

Vanunu never doubted that political pressure had ensured a guilty verdict. A few days later, he wrote:

All that I can say about my case is that justice was not done. I was in my trial with my lawyer and we knew that the judges just decided what someone else told them to do. Even the sentence is very unjust. So my hope is that the Supreme Court will say the truth in this case. There is one justice. I know the truth, and many people will one day see that the Government should have been convicted in this case, but the judges found the easy way by convicting me, and no one knew what happened in the trial. This is the way of the security service.

Vanunu assumed the Israeli Government had directed the judges to find him guilty, but legal experts inside Israel insisted there was no need to strong-arm the judges into a guilty verdict they would have reached by themselves.

Israel sets great store by its judicial apparatus. It is part of the democratic process that sets Israel apart from the totalitarian regimes of its enemies. The Government stood to do considerable damage by perverting that process to have Vanunu convicted. The authorities could count on the Zionist orientation of the judiciary, which had shown itself in the past to be highly responsive to what the Government considered were important security needs.

Throughout the trial, prosecutor Uzi Hasson had missed no opportunity to stress the security damage already done by Vanunu's disclosures, and the further damage threatened by allowing Vanunu access to the media. Without the judges' independence being compromised, it was reasonable to expect—as the British Government had clearly expected in the first Spycatcher trials in Britain—that the political conservatism of the judiciary would guarantee the desired verdict. With his characteristic naivety, Vanunu assumed that they had conspired to produce a guilty verdict.

Other aspects of the case made Vanunu's acquittal

unlikely. His support for a Palestinian homeland was anathema to millions of Jews—refugees from the Holocaust as well as those who had witnessed the near-disaster of the 1973 war—to whom the creation of a Palestinian State symbolised the first stage in the destruction of Israel.

Vanunu's moral justification for his actions was, for most Israelis, fatally compromised by his identification with the Arab cause. As Jonathan Kuttab, a Jerusalem lawyer and prominent civil rights activist, observed:

> The Israeli so-called peace force or moderate camp is in a constant state of defensiveness. They constantly have to show that they are not soft on matters of security, that they are in fact good solid Zionists and good nationalists. If an Israeli favours peace with the Palestinians or talks with the PLO or giving up of territories, he would be unlikely to come to the defence of someone like Vanunu, because he wouldn't want to be open to charges of being soft on vital national security interests at a time when he is trying to boost his credibility in order to make a statement on the Palestinian issue.

Kuttab described this dilemma as 'one of the classical problems of the leftist, moderate peace camp in Israel'. It was a weakness which ensured that the support Vanunu did gain for his actions against nuclear weapons was rarely heard.

Secondly, as the Israeli journalist Yael Lotan recognised, there were those who would never forgive Vanunu's desertion of his Jewish faith. There was no need for right-wing extremists in the Knesset to argue that Vanunu had been part of a Christian conspiracy against the Jews; for many his conversion was betrayal enough. Vanunu's decision to become a Christian was interpreted by these people not as a private act of faith, but as a betrayal of his heritage and, by extension, his country.

Uzi Hasson, the State prosecutor, illustrated this in cross-examination of Peter Hounam at Vanunu's trial. Hounam had flown to Israel to act as a defence witness during the proceedings. Asking Hounam if he had known that Vanunu had become a Christian when they met in Australia, Hounam replied that he had. 'Then,' said Hasson, 'you must have realised that he had turned away from his family and his country.' To Hounam, reporting the cross-examination in *The Sunday Times*, Hasson's comment was an 'apparent *non sequitur*'. He wondered if the Israeli prosecutor was joking. Hasson's statement demonstrated how Vanunu's religious conversion had been twisted into a patriotic issue, just as his moral argument against nuclear weapons had been submerged by the cry of treason.

After being found guilty, Vanunu wrote:

> God wants us to live in peace and nuclear weapons are not for peace. I could not stand in silent. It was my obligation to all the people to warned them. The judges put all my case in terms of spy-espionage not in terms of obeying my conscience. At least they can say that I was not spy, but everything in this country is going wrong. From the beginning they brought me against my will, against the international law, like any terrorist group. So if the government is doing terrorist actions, there cannot be justice.

Having secured a guilty verdict, and prevented any more details of Vanunu's abduction from reaching the public, the authorities seemed less interested in what he wrote in his letters. Where previously the word 'kidnap' had been scribbled out by the prison censor, it was now allowed to stand. Vanunu, turning his hopes to the Supreme Court judges who would hear his appeal, wrote about it obsessively:

> They put me in jail like a criminal man, and brought me here by terrorist action against all the human rights and against the law, and they put me in very bad prison conditions. Every day they reminding me how they kidnap

me. Every day they are kidnapping me from my cell to a small courtyard to walk one hour, but I'll not forget what they do to me and how they 'succeed' in their unjustice trial. ... Now I am waiting with patience to the Supreme Court. I believe that more worst that has happened, now only could be better.

By refusing to take into account the illegality of Vanunu's arrest, the District Court judges attempted to define the case as a purely domestic matter involving the violation of Israeli State secrets. But in spiriting Vanunu away from Rome, the Mossad had left the Italian Government with an embarrassing mystery on its hands. It had no wish to prove that Israeli agents had committed a crime on Italian soil, but could not be seen to ignore the well-publicised kidnap allegations.

The mystery was scarcely laid to rest by the release, in September 1988, of a long-awaited report by Domenico Sica. Sica, formerly Rome's public prosecutor, had by then been appointed as the Italian Government's special commissioner against the Mafia. He had a reputation for independence. Sica had said many times that he was determined to find out what happened to Vanunu after he flew into Fiumicino Airport on 30th September 1986, and vanished. Shortly before Vanunu was sentenced, Sica had declared: 'I am not concerned with whether or not Vanunu has been found guilty. What has to be cleared up is how he ended up in Israel. We shall see how this issue is treated in the sentence hearing.'

Although the Israeli Government had made it clear from the start that he would not be allowed to see Vanunu, Sica had promised a vigorous investigation. Yet after an inquiry lasting more than a year, Sica reached the surprising and impossible conclusion that Vanunu had not been kidnapped, but had been involved in an elaborate piece of 'mystification'.

Sica's report, which ran to seven pages, concluded

that 'the entire affair reveals such bizarre and contradictory aspects as to lead to the conclusion that fundamentally it involves a well-organised disinformation operation, aimed at introducing—in interested quarters—a patrimony of information in all likelihood false or altered with respect to reality.'

Sica deduced that the whole operation, from taking the photographs inside Dimona to Vanunu's kidnap in Rome, was organised by the Mossad. But Sica's report contained its own mysteries: in a story riddled with contradictions, Sica had chosen the least contentious elements on which to build his conclusions. With doubt undermining every part of the story, Sica had manufactured his own mysteries based on reckless assumptions and simple misreadings of the available evidence.

Some of Sica's doubts seemed the result of obtuseness. He remarked that Vanunu, ever since his first contact with *The Sunday Times*, had lived and travelled under a succession of false identities, usually based around his baptismal name. When he left Britain on BA flight 504, Vanunu was travelling under his own name. This, Sica thought, seemed to indicate that Vanunu was leaving an obvious trail from the exact area of his disappearance.

As with virtually every other interpretation of Vanunu's story, this suggestion is impossible to refute. There are, however, more plausible explanations. Vanunu was a courageous man, but not a fool. The passport he carried and all the personal documents he had with him were filled out in his own name. By masquerading as a European Community citizen, Vanunu might hope to avoid showing his passport, but he could not depend upon it with certainty. If he were made to show his passport when travelling under a false identity, the discrepancy would show up immediately. By travelling under his real identity, Vanunu at least saved himself the trouble of such obvious—and futile—deceits.

The question of Cindy's identity is more perplexing. The passenger manifest obtained by *The Sunday Times* showed that the seat next to Vanunu's had been occupied by 'C. Hanin'. As Sica correctly points out, her perfunctory change of name—from Cheryl to Cindy—did nothing to disguise her presence, since only the initials are used on an airline ticket. It took more than a year, but *The Sunday Times* finally tracked down Cindy to an address in Netanya, Israel, where she lived with her husband, a major in the Israeli secret service. Why she took so little trouble to hide her identity was certainly mysterious. Sica concluded that she was 'ingenuous'.

Sica had been presented with Meir Vanunu's detailed account of the kidnapping in Rome. He was suspicious of the way Meir claimed to have obtained it from his brother in prison, stating that 'the declarations of Meir Vanunu are obviously second-hand ... one cannot see how juducial, prison or police authorities as severe and restrictive as the Israeli ones described by [Meir] Vanunu himself to the PM [Public Minister, ie Sica] should then allow their prisoner to recount compromising details, but understandably never complete or details really useful for the deepening of any type of investigation'. The declarations Meir made to Sica were described as suffering from 'simplifications that render them even more untenable'. In a statement disarmingly reminiscent of many made about Vanunu himself, Sica went on to make the damning accusation that Meir had been moved to speak 'only by the economic contribution of *The Sunday Times*'.

Sica was particularly concerned about Meir's claim that Vanunu had been taken to a cheap apartment block in Rome, drugged by Israeli agents and then carried out to a waiting van. 'The third floor of a council house ... is the most unsuitable and dangerous place from which to remove an unconscious body,' Sica wrote.

'It goes without saying that a group of experts would never have made a similar mistake. Just the same as the methods of immobilisation and the subsequent administration of a soporific substance are clearly romanticised.'

In this Sica shows a curious naivety about the skills of the Mossad which, almost twenty years before, had manhandled the doped and barely conscious Adolf Eichmann past Argentine customs officials and onto a commercial airliner back to Israel. The task of escorting a co-operatively inert body down a few flights of stairs and onto the street of one of the world's busiest cities would seem a far less hazardous venture.

Apart from Sica's somewhat idiosyncratic interpretations of available evidence, he made some extraordinary errors of fact, leading inevitably to serious misrepresentations of crucial parts of the story.

One of these concerns the palm message. On the first page of his report, Sica wrote:

Vanunu reappeared the following November 9 in Israel, with just enough time to allow himself to be photographed while riding in a glass-enclosed van that transported him to the courthouse to be tried for espionage. On that occasion and in the only photograph taken, evidently with exceptional timing and the great fortune of having avoided the reflection from the glass against which it was supported, the technician succeeded in showing the palm of his hand on which was written the phrase: 'I was kidnapped in Rome 30.9.1986, 21.00 hours. Arrived in Rome from London on flight BA504.'

Commenting on the message as he had recorded it, Sica noted that 'the text is written in correct English; Vanunu's letters are normally written in a rather approximate English and even surrender to elementary errors.'

Here, Sica is quite correct. Vanunu's letters are littered with grammatical errors and words unique to himself: 'humanbeing' for humanity, 'hungry strike' for hunger strike and many others. But the message he quotes is not the message Vanunu wrote.

The actual message written on Vanunu's palm—'Vanunu M WAS HIJACKEN IN ROME ITL, 30.9.86 21.00, Came to Rome BY BA FLY 504'—is not the flawless statement quoted by Sica. The original words were displayed on hundreds of newspaper photographs all over the world, yet Sica drew his conclusions from a misquoted version.

Sica's assumption that the one photo which appeared in the newspapers was the only one taken is tendentious. As reports of the incident showed, the van was besieged by photographers, most of whom, no doubt, had loaded cameras. The fact that one image represented the moment more clearly than any other testifies rather to the bad timing and misfortune of all the other photographs, than to the 'exceptional timing and great fortune' of the successful picture.

Sica's last query is the only one which reaches to the heart of the Vanunu mystery. It concerns the photographs he showed *The Sunday Times*:

Finally, Vanunu deposited into the hands of *The Sunday Times* reporters a sequence of photographs that he took by himself with a normal camera, shots of the exterior straight through to the most sensitive recesses of the Dimona atomic factory.

The photographs were again shown to an expert in nuclear science. In a footnote to the report, Sica wrote:

The expert expressed the following opinion about the photographs he was shown: 'The photographs in negatives 1 through 6 represent the exterior of nuclear facilities; in particular negatives 1, 2 and 6 show the exterior of the Dimona reactor. The photos 7 to 18 and from 19 to 46 represent a combustible radiation treatment facility in a nuclear reactor [nuclear waste treatment facility], to separate the various elements present in the waste itself;

from this type of facility it is possible to extract from the waste—in particular plutonium, which can be utilised as nuclear explosive; various photographs represent different phases of the extraction process. Photos 47 to 52 show part of the construction process and samples of the product, metallic spheres of various shapes and dimensions typical of nuclear explosives attached to external shells of a material that appears to be graphite. It cannot yet be established if the metal of the spheres is in fact plutonium. The sequence of the above-indicated photos corresponds with the logical order to follow (production of material, separation of fissionable material, production of the explosive device) to obtain a nuclear device.

It was the interpretation of these photographs, Sica declared, that 'above all ... gives the tranquil certainty that in reality the entire affair is nothing but a mystification'.

This 'certainty' is based—as was his comment on Cindy's half-hearted disguise—not on proof, but on probability. Without producing any fresh evidence, Sica dismisses the whole case on the ground of scepticism. In summing up the photographs, Sica proves only that the truth remained as elusive as ever:

There is no doubt that the photographs correspond with true images of an atomic plant; it is rather likely that they really correspond to the atomic plant of Dimona in Israel: this results from what was said by the office-appointed expert [ie, the expert commissioned by the Public Minister's office to investigate the photographs]. The aspect of the affair which is objectively incredible, however, is based on the fact that the photographs constitute a rigorously chronological series of a visit to the plant, which opens with a panoramic external view to another panoramic view of the facilities seen from inside the gates, to an exposure of all the various productive sectors, excluding none, ending with a contemplation of the atomic devices assembled and disassembled and in various angles. A sequence of a rather guided-tour nature of the said exposé defies the test of logic and goes against the regime of security and compartmental-isation that surely is enforced at the Dimona plant (for obvious reasons of technological secrecy and evident security motives against terrorist attack). No one can deem possible, not even a technician, taking photographs one after the other, even with the use of a flash, up to the heart of the atomic plant without encountering any difficulty. That is if it is not done with the consensus of those interested: this could explain the fact that in all of the examined negatives (including the panoramic shots taken from far away) any kind of human presence is never revealed. Looking at the Dimona plant through Vanunu's 'photographic service' it would seem to be a totally deserted one.... Nor can it be claimed that the photos were taken during a holiday or after working hours: as the office-appointed expert immedi-ately brought to light in his report, at Dimona high-risk work is carried out during absolutely continuous cycles that do not consent any working pause; and the instrumentation and monitors opportunely photographed by Vanunu require constant attention and intervention on the part of numer-ous personnel.

In all this, Sica's doubts are essentially the same as those put forward by *The Sunday Times* in its original report. Of the scientists contacted by the paper, several were highly sceptical of the way Vanunu claimed to have obtained his photographs, although the majority was prepared to accept the explanation that in such a dangerous plant, unrestricted movement and free access were essential for certain technicians in order to deal promptly with any malfunction.

As a result of being interviewed by the authorities over his pro-Palestinian activities, Vanunu knew that he would be made redundant. He was resentful, but he also wanted to take a record of what he had been doing. As Peter Hounam described it, there was 'an element of bitterness about Vanunu's determination to get the photographs'. At the time he was taking the photographs, Vanunu had been working at Dimona for

nine years. Even in a top-secret installation like
Machon 2, such familiarity must have made the security
guards and other employees lax in their enforcement of
security procedures.

Vanunu had, at any rate, taken precautions in the
event of being discovered. He had brought the camera
and film in separately in a bag full of books. If the
camera had been found in a random search, he planned
to say that he had taken it to the beach and forgotten to
remove it. Operations at Dimona were largely auto-
matic, and there were no closed-circuit cameras to
observe Vanunu as he snatched photographs of all the
key sections of the plant. When he had finished, Vanunu
smuggled out the empty camera in exactly the same
way he had brought it in.

Vanunu's action required luck and careful planning.
His success begs the question of how security could have
been so negligent, and leaves open the possibility that
the authorities at Dimona, having discovered what
Vanunu was doing, decided not to stop him. But it
falls some way short of proving Sica's conclusion that
the entire affair was a 'well-organised disinformation
campaign'.

In fact, the report is riddled with legal references
suggesting that the purpose of Sica's investigation was
not to clear up 'how [Vanunu] ended up in Israel' but
to establish that Italian laws had not been broken
in getting him there. 'The affair encompasses some
elements of such untenableness,' he wrote, 'as to lead to
the conclusion that the kidnapping never occurred at all
or that it occurred elsewhere and therefore nothing of
penal relevance occurred in Italy.' Sica even added in a
footnote that 'the British authorities never seemed to
occupy themselves with the episode that, in any case,
even if by deception and without violence, was initiated
on English territory'.

The concluding paragraph of Sica's report leaves the

distinct impression that the thrust of the inquiry was less to establish the truth, than to absolve the Italian Government of legal jurisdiction. 'The PM,' Sica wrote, 'in the impossibility of obtaining and evaluating ulterior elements of proof, is of the opinion that penal action lacks proof—there being no demonstration that crimes were committed on Italian territory—and therefore requests that the Investigating Magistrate, in his office, orders the transfer of the acts to the archives.'

Sica's report thus served an identical purpose to the perfunctory investigations by the British police of what happened in London. The Italian Government, like the British Government, was content to sweep the Vanunu affair under the thick carpet of international diplomacy.

The most intriguing aspect of Sica's investigation was not the evidence it threw up, but the evidence it left out. What information he did have, he seemed wilfully to bend out of shape with his bizarre interpretations and curious omissions. Had Sica made a serious attempt to follow the story outside Italy, he would have run up against more plausible evidence for his claim of a disinformation campaign. He would certainly have wanted to know more about the extraordinary coincidence that put Oscar Guerrero on the scene at precisely the moment Vanunu was considering telling his story, and why this should have happened in Australia, of all places.

Sica also failed to query the value of the leaked information. Middle-East commentators pointed out that the news of Israel's military invulnerability would severely embarrass its Arab enemies. The leak itself, however, was hardly new: journalists all over the world, and particularly in the United States, had taken it for granted that Israel possessed a powerful nuclear deterrent. Richard Sale, in the US magazine *Aerospace Daily*, had reported in 1985 that Israel might have as many as

200 nuclear weapons, and had already deployed them on its Jericho II missiles. Vanunu's disclosures had provided the details to substantiate Sale's report, as well as revealing Israel's capacity to build thermonuclear weapons and the neutron bomb. The kidnapping and jailing of Vanunu gave credibility to claims that the story was a damaging leak. Clearly Israel stood to benefit from having its military strength confirmed by a respected newspaper like *The Sunday Times*, while the Government maintained its pose of denying the truth of the leak. Such a scam would explain why Vanunu was able to take the photographs and why he was allowed to carry them out of the country, but it cannot explain why Israel took such risks to get him back. It presumes a reckless confidence, unlikely in the light of earlier blunders, that the Mossad would leave no incriminating clues behind, and an improbable reliance on luck and the willingness of its allies to ride out the political storm surrounding the abduction.

It is possible that the Israelis discovered what Vanunu was doing and let him get away with it in the belief that Israel could only profit from the revelations. The evidence for this is as speculative as the evidence against it, except that here the theory encounters the mercurial figure of Oscar Guerrero, who delivered the story to *The Sunday Times*. Roland Selicus, Guerrero's fence-painting partner, remembered Vanunu telling him one day that he wanted to burn the photographs and forget everything. It was Guerrero's persistence that refused to let the story die, yet Guerrero's appearance at St John's was entirely coincidental. Guerrero had been sent to St John's to paint a fence as part of a government-sponsored employment scheme. Although the local employment office had selected Guerrero, it was left to John McKnight to accept or reject him. It is beyond belief that an organisation as clinical as the Mossad would plan such a complex operation around a coincidence.

Despite the vast amount of newsprint that has been expended on the kidnapping, nobody—least of all Domenico Sica—has thrown up any evidence that Vanunu was a party to a deliberate Israeli disinformation campaign. Meanwhile, the impossibility of seeing Vanunu in jail and the resolute silence of the Israeli Government have effectively blocked any evidence against it. Sica's conclusion that Vanunu was part of a Mossad conspiracy must carry with it the assumption that Vanunu is either not in prison at all or—even more absurdly—that he agreed to go to prison. During all his time in Ashkelon Prison, Vanunu has only been seen when he was presented for viewing. Only once—during a visit by Avigdor Feldman—was he caught unawares, sleeping in his cell. Yet his conviction and eighteen-year prison sentence, as well as the determination of the security services to stop him speaking about what happened, leave little doubt that Vanunu was silenced against his will.

The most compelling evidence against the conspiracy theory comes from Vanunu himself, both in his letters and in the impression he made on the people who knew him. Neither Peter Hounam, who spent more than five weeks talking regularly with Vanunu, nor his brother Meir, nor anyone at St John's, has any doubt that Vanunu's motives for telling his story were genuine. For Sica's conclusion to be right, all the people who knew him must be wrong.

His letters supply equally strong evidence about his motives and the reality of his imprisonment. Vanunu writes too passionately, too mundanely and too repetitively to be a convincing fraud. He complains three times about being slandered by his former supporter Benjamin Merhav from Melbourne, scarcely a significant figure in the story. He writes with a fervour for details and a certainty of his own ill-treatment that defies the interpretation Sica imposes on it.

CHAPTER FOURTEEN

WHATEVER THE INTENTIONS OF THE SICA INQUIRY, the outcome was incomplete and unsatisfactory, submerging the broader issues raised by the kidnap beneath the more pressing needs of political expediency. As Peter Hounam saw it: 'Italy has dragged its feet over the whole affair. It has taken eighteen months to produce a shallow and inaccurate report that doesn't begin to address the central point of Vanunu being hijacked, as he stated quite clearly on his hand message.'

Vanunu himself, describing his trial, had told McKnight: 'They did not want to hear me, to believe me and to understand what I did. They convict me like a spy, and even more than spy, and all what I did is publish those secrets that should not be hidden from the people about nuclear dangers.'

He was referring to the trial judges, but the description might easily have fitted the Italian investigators, the British police, the Israeli Government or any of the other officials who were unable 'to hear ... to believe ... and to understand' Vanunu. The Sica report was merely one more attempted explanation of Vanunu's actions to place alongside the earlier ones. In each case, they distorted or failed to understand or simply refused to acknowledge the reasons that lay behind Vanunu's actions. Perhaps this was inevitable. The officials called upon to investigate and explain Vanunu's behaviour were both symbols and servants of the authority that Vanunu himself had defied.

In breaking the laws that bound him to secrecy, Vanunu denied the legitimacy of those laws and the Government that enforced them. His actions represented an appeal to individual consciences over the heads of Governments and politicians, a repudiation of the bogus community of the State in favour of a Stateless community based on conscience and shared moral convictions. The values he preached were the values of Christ, but the roots of such an appeal lay deep in his Jewish heritage. Unique among modern nations, the State of Israel is defined solely by its Jewish beliefs. While it was natural for Israelis to cast Vanunu the Christian convert as a traitor, it was also natural for Vanunu, as a former Jew, to appeal to a spiritual community that transcended its natural origins. His challenge was not only to the Government of Israel, but to all governments everywhere.

It is the same like the case of Peter Write [Peter Wright, author of *Spycatcher*] who publish his book in Australia and no one kidnapped him and put him in jail. This is the different between democratic country and this country.... For me I did the right thing and I believe that my action help to prevent nuclear war in this region and what happen to me and my suffering is the same like many people who suffer for their conscience, and we have the example of Jesus who died for us. So this example make easier my suffering, and now after two years I am very happy to know that those who put me in this golak [gulag] solitary confinement, they didn't succeed to break my soul, my faith, and will not succeed to separate me from Jesus Christ our Lord.

Peter Wright's legal victory against the British Government emphasises the illegality of what was done to Vanunu. But the similarities of the two cases are more fundamental than the differences. Wright and Vanunu both used their positions to obtain classified information. Both violated what the State declared to be official secrets. The Thatcher Government did its utmost to prevent Wright from publishing information it considered harmful to Britain's interests, and pursued a vindictive and dishonest campaign against him through the courts of Britain and Australia. In 1985, the British Government had shown similar determination to convict and punish Clive Ponting, a high-ranking adviser in the Ministry of Defence who had leaked secret information about the Falklands War, but was again defeated by the courts. Fortunately for Peter Wright and for Clive Ponting, the British Government did not have the same licence to apprehend and punish its critics as the Israeli Government allowed itself in kidnapping Vanunu.

After the Ponting trial, the British commentator Robin Oakley wrote: 'The case was designed to deter civil servants from putting their own consciences above the instructions of their political masters.'[27] The same statement could be applied to the prosecution of Mordechai Vanunu, only in Vanunu's case the court sided with the Government.

Vanunu argued that his duty to his conscience surpassed his duty to the authority of the State. He had spent nine years working behind the electrified wire and guns of Dimona, a party to the secrecy that shrouded Israel's development of nuclear weapons. He understood that the nuclear world, by necessity, was one of ever-diminishing democratic freedoms, because nuclear technology was too sophisticated and too deadly to allow proper democratic supervision. He believed that in the face of official duplicity, it was the right of the individual to demand information. By providing that information, Vanunu violated the secret consensus which had governed Israel's nuclear build-up for thirty years, a consensus involving not just the Israelis themselves, but their American allies and the international watchdogs entrusted with preventing the proliferation of nuclear weapons.

Vanunu had lived through the 1973 war, when Israel had had to fight for its life against an Arab invasion, and had heard the bellicose speeches of Arab warmongers such as Gadaffi and Hussein. He recognised the tacit approval within Israel that allowed successive Israeli Governments to pursue a nuclear weapons programme unopposed, but he called on the Israeli people to throw out a democratic contract based on deceit and the suppression of truth. Vanunu disputed the right of any democratic Government to carry out its policies in secret. He was condemned for espionage, but his crime was disobedience.

About disobedience he wrote,

> I believe that in this case about the nuclear issue and the secrets, someone had to do the same as I did. I didn't do it for any government. All I did was give information that I believe has to become known to the citizens of this country. In some cases I think we can break the law. In the case of the Holocaust in Germany, if someone broke the law he was considered a worthy man because he wanted to prevent the Holocaust. And what do I want? In the nuclear issue everywhere in the world, what we can do is to be aware of their perils, and to express our fears. Nuclear weapons are not for human hands. They put too much power in one button. No country should have the destructive power which nuclear weapons bring. I believe many people know about those dangers. How could I forget and forgive myself if I didn't do it. The main point was that I knew if I didn't do what I did, no one else was going to do it, so I took the risk and sacrificed my freedom for it until my release.

Vanunu never accepted the State's definition of him as a criminal. He believed he had made his protest in the only way open to him. 'My action was for saving life,' he wrote. 'Is it bad to save life? I didn't harm anyone. This is the truth. It is not disobedience in the nuclear issue. We all human beings will die by the foolish scientists and Government.'

For Vanunu, breaking what he believed to be an immoral law was not merely a legitimate act of protest, but a duty to his fellow human beings. 'I could not stand in silent,' he wrote to McKnight. 'It was my obligation.... I am not a traitor. If I had not spoken then I was a traitor.'

Vanunu's sense of obligation meant more than just moral conviction. It was bound up with faith, and the duty to follow God's will without question. 'I didn't want to do what I have done,' he wrote, 'but God chose me because there was no one else who could do what I have done.'

Obligation, as Vanunu understood it, was not the absence of choice, but the necessity of choice. He took the idea from Kierkegaard. In *Fear and Trembling*, Kierkegaard had employed the biblical story of Abraham to illustrate the ultimate challenge of faith. This was the only one of Kierkegaard's books to have been translated into Hebrew and the only one Vanunu had read before coming to Australia. David Smith recalls it playing a key role in the philosophical discussions he had with Vanunu at St John's:

The idea of the individual having the courage to make a decision alone and taking responsibility for the things you do was very much a part of Mordechai's understanding of Christianity and the course of action he consequently took. It is significant that *Fear and Trembling* is about the story of Abraham, where Abraham is asked to go and murder his son. Kierkegaard says that this is the knight of faith—the one who is willing to do something not only against his own interests but even against his own morality, and is willing to take a stand because he knows God has called him to do this. For Kierkegaard this is the essence of faith because it distinguishes it from duty. Morde believed in the idea of being totally alone in making decisions and willing to take on the full responsibility yourself.

After Vanunu was imprisoned, the sense of personal responsibility assumed an overwhelming importance. The knowledge of having taken the decision alone became a source of strength for him now that he was physically isolated and powerless. His rejection of support from those with other political commitments now signified something deeper than mistrust. It represented a demand for purity of responsibility, a striving after spiritual solitude in which his model was Christ himself.

> I, as Jesus, my action was to serve others. A servant of all. Jesus gave up his life for the sake of the people who put him to death. So in my case in all my time here during my suffering I am looking on Jesus Christ's life. God appeared on earth in human form. Not only did he not sacrifice human beings for his sake but he suffered a lonely, anguishing, degrading human death so that the world might be saved. This thought is from the book of Jonathan Schell [*The Fate of the Earth*]. If Jesus was in this time—the nuclear time—he also would do as he has done, to give his life to save the world from the perils of nuclear weapons. The danger of nuclear weapons is that we cannot let the nuclear holocaust occur. We have to do our best to prevent this future. Nuclear weapons are not for defence, they are for extinction. They have no right to possess this weapon and to threaten with it. We have come to live on borrowed time. Every year of continued human life on earth is a borrowed year, every day a borrowed day. Now we have to save our earth, our future, the future of all mankind.

During the months after his trial, Vanunu seemed perversely determined to shake off his old supporters. 'Now I don't have any friends or any supporters,' he told McKnight. 'I don't need anyone.' In one letter he even warned McKnight to beware of Jewish infiltrators joining his own church:

I want to tell you that you have to be careful with all the new people who came to St John's. It could be that some of them they came to create quarles [quarrels] and to spread my friends from St John's and they are not Christian at all. This the kind of security service work.

There was something puzzling about Vanunu's need to rid himself of those with other political allegiances, as if his solitude had become self-serving. McKnight knew that many of those disowned by Vanunu were still lobbying on his behalf, but Vanunu would not be convinced. Like his hunger strikes, and his refusal for months to leave his cell, the rejection of those who were striving for his release combined self-destructiveness with a need to exert the little power still left to him in jail.

The act of cutting himself off from his Jewish supporters also served another purpose. Vanunu was now able to focus his hopes on the one community with which he could identify completely: the congregation of St John's. Vanunu wrote incessantly of his time at St John's, requesting tape recordings of the Sunday morning service, asking to be remembered to all the parishioners and members of staff who knew him.

'I would like to know about all what is going on at St John's,' he wrote. 'St John's Church is the place where I was born again, the place where I find the Lord Jesus Christ my Lord and my God, and I'll wait until the day that we will praise the Lord and give thanks.'

Convinced that his Jewish family could never accept his conversion, Vanunu looked for sanctuary in his memories of St John's, unaware of some of the divisions within the congregation over its support for him. He appealed constantly to his 'brothers and sisters at St John's', hoping that 'everything in St John's is well, the study group, the coffee shop'. He was distraught when one of the parishioners told him that Stephen Gray was moving to another church. 'It is very bad indeed to know that Father Steve leaved St John's parish,' he told

McKnight. 'I hope and pray for him that he will enjoy his new church.'

Vanunu had told David Smith that his ambition was one day to be an altar server at St John's. Now he spoke of his ambition to become a priest once he was allowed to return. Fixed in his memory, the congregation symbolised an ideal community of the human spirit in which he could immerse himself totally, and from which his enemies could never separate him. 'I would like to receive any letters from them and pictures,' he wrote. 'I know that some of them have written to me, but the Jews here they don't want that I'll keep my faith, but they cannot succeed, because God is with us and no one can be against us.'

Throughout his imprisonment, Vanunu has fought a ceaseless battle not to be forgotten, not to allow himself, like Domenico Sica's report, to be consigned to the archives. His hand held up to the window of the prison van signified moral defiance because Israel had no legal right to kidnap him, but also—and more important—it signified a refusal to be silenced. Having told the world about Israel's nuclear weapons, Vanunu now called on the world to judge him, and to judge the Government that brought him to trial.

All I want is that the people have the right to know what is going on in this issue. Only an international court can say if all that I did is for peace and my obligation to the humanbeing, and if the Israeli Government's actions are against the law. But now my judges are part of the Israeli Government and I have to convince them that I did the right thing to do, and that this government is going the wrong way and that the citizens have the right to know about the nuclear issue in this country.

Israel refused and still refuses to be judged, either for its clandestine development of nuclear weapons or for its illegal abduction of Vanunu. It maintains a strict silence on both, punctuated with disingenuous and evasive denials.

Ehud Olmert, a member of the conservative Likud Party then sitting on the foreign affairs and security committee of Parliament, defended the supposedly imaginary kidnapping with a panache that served only to emphasise the Government's ducking of the moral issue:

> Not everything is justifiable in self-defence, but bringing to court a traitor is, in my mind, an elementary obligation of a State towards its own security and to its citizens. If Israel did what was necessary under those circumstances without breaking the laws of other countries, I think it was absolutely in place and I commend those who had the courage of taking those decisions and those who had the ingenuity and resourcefulness of executing those decisions.[28]

The Israeli Government has continued to insist that 'at no stage will Israel be the first country in the Middle East to introduce nuclear weapons', as if Vanunu had never spoken. At the same time, it has persisted in painting him as a criminal and distorting the motives behind his actions. In June 1990, President Chaim Herzog replied to an open letter by the editor of *The Sunday Times*, Andrew Neil, calling on him to pardon Vanunu. In his reply, Herzog declared that 'Mordechai Vanunu was not convicted for his anti-nuclear views, nor for an act of conscience. He was convicted for revealing classified information with a clear intent to impair Israel's security.'

Vanunu had no such intent. He never questioned Israel's right to defend itself, only its right to defend itself with nuclear weapons, which he saw as a threat to the whole of humanity. 'The nuclear danger', he wrote, 'is too important to leave it in the hands of politicians. I believe everyone in this world has to do all that he can to make life better for all human beings.' Vanunu saw nuclear weapons as an issue that concerned not just Israelis, but all people. A nuclear explosion, whether it happens by accident or intent, has no respect for national boundaries.

> I believe that more people in every country will know more about the danger, and one day we will be free from this threat. This is my message – to be free from the nuclear threat. And how can we be free? The first step is to know about them, to know the existence of the danger. That was my act – to let everyone know. The knowledge we gain by my actions prepares us to do our best against this danger.

Vanunu understood that without knowledge there could be no discussion and no eradication of nuclear weapons. 'The first step against nuclear perils is to know about them', he wrote in one of his earliest letters from prison. 'To know is to be responsible.'

Vanunu argued during his trial that ordinary Israelis had the right to know the strength of their country's nuclear arsenal because the next Arab-Israeli conflict could end in nuclear war. 'Our hope is that one day we will be free from nuclear weapons on earth', he said. 'The way is to sign a nuclear moratorium for a non-proliferation treaty all over the earth, or to destroy all the nuclear weapons in this region.'

On 27th May 1990, Vanunu was taken from his cell in Ashkelon Prison to Jerusalem's Supreme Court to hear the result of his appeal. He was brought before the court in manacles and leg chains. It took just five minutes for Israel's Chief Justice, Meir Shamgar, to dispose of more than a hundred legal arguments put forward in his defence by his lawyer, Avigdor Feldman. 'The appeal against the sentence and verdict is rejected', he said. Soon afterwards, Shamgar and two other appeal judges left the court.

In less than two hours, Vanunu was back in solitary confinement in the tiny cell where he had spent the past four years of his life. On the wall, near a small crucifix, was a map of Sydney he had pinned up to remind him of the place where he began the action that robbed him of his freedom.

Vanunu remained defiant. 'Keep your thoughts about me. I feel very good', he said. 'I'm strong enough to wait until my release.'

Feldman announced that he would go on fighting for Vanunu's release, but would now turn his efforts to improving the conditions of imprisonment, especially his solitary confinement, which he feared might affect Vanunu's sanity.

A few days later, Vanunu wrote to David Smith in Sydney:

> It is not only that I have received 18 years, but they say that everything is good in the nuclear issue in this country, that the people here don't have to know anything about nuclear issues. It is not only that they condemn me in spying but said that all my actions was not necessary and no word about their unlawful action in the way to bring me here. This is the injustice of this democratic country.

Since I was baptised into union
with Christ Jesus I became a free man.

Mordechai Vanunu
Ashkelon Prison

EPILOGUE

THE GULF WAR OF 1990 THREW INTO STARK RELIEF the catastrophic risks involved in having weapons of mass destruction in the Middle East. Just months earlier, Iraq's President Saddam Hussein had vowed to 'let our fire eat half of Israel if it tries to wage anything against Iraq . . . He who threatens us with an atomic bomb will be annihilated by binary chemicals.'

During the Gulf War, Saddam's attempts to drag Israel into the fighting by raining Scud missiles down on its cities failed to provoke Israeli retaliation. Had it succeeded, the brittle alliance against Iraq might have collapsed and the war might have escalated far beyond its original confines. But the possibility that the Israeli leadership might have been compelled, for political or military reasons, to respond to Iraq's provocations remained real enough. The presence of nuclear weapons, whether their use against Iraq was envisaged or not, inevitably raised the stakes.

The danger of nuclear proliferation in the Middle East and throughout the world remains acute. The end of the Cold War has, if anything, made the risk of nuclear war greater. Control of the former Soviet Union's huge nuclear arsenal has passed into the hands of governments whose hold on power is often tenuous. Some are bogged down in ethnic disputes which have the potential to erupt into open warfare. Porous borders have made it harder to stop nuclear materials reaching the black market.

The former Soviet republics cannot afford to dismantle their nuclear arsenals without vast amounts of Western aid. Distrust of Russian intentions has prevented smaller republics from surrendering their weapons. Terrorist acquisition of plutonium is always a threat.

The festering dispute over Kashmir continues to poison relations between India and Pakistan, both of which have advanced nuclear weapons programmes. Potentially the gravest threat of all comes from North Korea, whose persistent sabre-rattling and bellicose refusal to allow unrestricted international inspection of its nuclear facilities have dangerously heightened tensions in the region.

Meanwhile Mordechai Vanunu's own situation stays the same. The election of a new Labour government in Israel has failed to secure any significant improvement in Vanunu's conditions. While Israel inches towards peace with both the Palestinians and Syria, Vanunu remains where he has been since 1986, in solitary confinement, a so-called threat to Israeli security.

Relentless political campaigning by his supporters around the world has so far had no success in convincing Israel's leaders that his continued imprisonment is an anomaly in a country which is gradually re-orienting itself towards accommodation with its traditional enemies.

Accounts from his lawyer and members of his family – the only visitors Vanunu is allowed under the stringent conditions of his imprisonment – have prompted fears for his sanity, with both describing Vanunu as 'closing himself off from the world'.

In a lengthy report on his incarceration, the human rights organisation Amnesty International listed many physical and psychological disorders associated with long-term solitary confinement. They included emotional disturbance, impairment of concentration and ability to think, loss of reality, neuroses, headaches and sleep disturbances.

Last year, Israel's Prime Minister, Yitzhak Rabin, made a request to the American President, Bill Clinton, for executive clemency for Jonathan Pollard, the American Jew convicted of spying for Israel in 1987 and sentenced to life imprisonment.

Pollard, a civilian intelligence analyst for the US Navy in the 1980s, had been recruited by the Israeli defence department to supply military intelligence, including satellite photos and information on Arab military systems. His severe sentence, like Vanunu's, was clearly intended as a deterrent, since there was little Pollard could do to jeopardise American security beyond what he had already done.

What Rabin has requested on Pollard's behalf, Israel's President Ezer Weizman is capable of reciprocating in the case of Mordechai Vanunu. The easing of Vanunu's conditions, and even his early release, would not be out of place in the changing Middle Eastern order. Israel has already shown a willingness to relax its hard line on security matters by releasing hundreds of Palestinian prisoners as a conciliatory gesture to the Palestinian Liberation Organisation. The release of Pollard in response to Rabin's personal request would improve Rabin's standing at home and strengthen his hand against those Israelis who oppose any compromise with the PLO.

Israeli security officials would not welcome any reduction in Vanunu's sentence any more than their American counterparts would welcome clemency for Pollard. But both acts would signal a readiness to let bygones be bygones in the wider interests of peace in the Middle East.

For having the courage to tell the truth about his

country's nuclear weapons, Vanunu suffered not just the punishment of an Israeli court, but the misunderstanding and opprobrium of his own people. He is still misunderstood and misrepresented, because the Israeli Government has denied him the right to explain his actions, preferring to cast him as a traitor efficiently brought to justice. In this role he offers a sober warning to others not to attempt the same thing.

Olof Palme, the murdered Swedish Prime Minister, declared in 1982 that in a nuclear world, safety could exist only in common security and the recognition of interdependence. He saw that the world was too small to hold so many conflicting nationalisms, any one of which, in the age of nuclear arms, could end in nuclear war. New nationalisms have broken out since then, fomented by leaders unconstrained by the loyalties and obligations of the Cold War. Vanunu recognised the truth in both Palme's statements. It was his crime to act on them.

Notes

1. 'France admits it gave Israel A-bomb', *The Sunday Times* (12th October 1986).
2. Michael Bar-Zohar, *Ben-Gurion, A Biography* (London, 1978), p 270.
3. 'France admits it gave Israel A-bomb', *The Sunday Times* (12th October 1986).
4. James Adams, *The Unnatural Alliance* (London, 1984), p 149.
5. Michael Bar-Zohar, *op cit* p 272.
6. David Ben-Gurion, *Israel: A Personal History* (Tel Aviv, 1971), p 660.
7. *Ibid* p 659.
8. Gary Milhollin, 'Heavy Water Cheaters', *Foreign Policy*, number 69.
9. Article by Howard Kohn and Barbara Newman, *Rolling Stone* (1st December 1977).
10. Elaine Davenport, Paul Eddy and Peter Gilman, *The Plumbat Affair* (London, 1978).
11. *Science* magazine, no 183 (22nd March 1974) p 1172.
12. Gary Milhollin, *op cit*.
13. *Ibid*.
14. *Newsweek* (22nd June 1981).
15. Conor Cruise O'Brien, *The Siege* (London, 1986), p 611.
16. *Sydney Sun* (9th May 1969).
17. *The Australian* (30th January 1978).
18. 'How Israel Got the Bomb', *Time* (12th April 1976).
19. Leonard S. Spector, *Going Nuclear* (Cambridge, Mass, 1987) p 293.
20. *Ibid* p 139.
21. Jane Hunter, *Israeli Foreign Policy – South Africa and Central America* (Boston, 1987), p 36.
22. *The Australian* (27th October 1979).
23. *Inquiry* (April 1980).
24. *The Independent* (30th June 1990).
25. 'The Dimona Factor', *Four Corners* (ABC Television, 31st August 1987).
26. English translation by Vivienne Heston.
27. *Sydney Morning Herald* (13th February 1985).
28. 'The Dimona Factor', *Four Corners* (ABC Television).